Our American Century

★

The Jazz Age · The 20s

★

By the Editors of Time-Life Books, Alexandria, Virginia

Contents

★

A busy throng of pedestrians and traffic crowd the corner of Fifth Avenue and 42nd Street, New York, 1926.

Doing the Charleston, three teams in St. Louis compete—with varying degrees of enthusiasm—in front of City Hall during a 1925 dance contest.

As increasing numbers of Americans take to the highway, roadside stands like this one proliferate, causing Ohio's Health Department to warn motorists to "be sure the drinking water is safe."

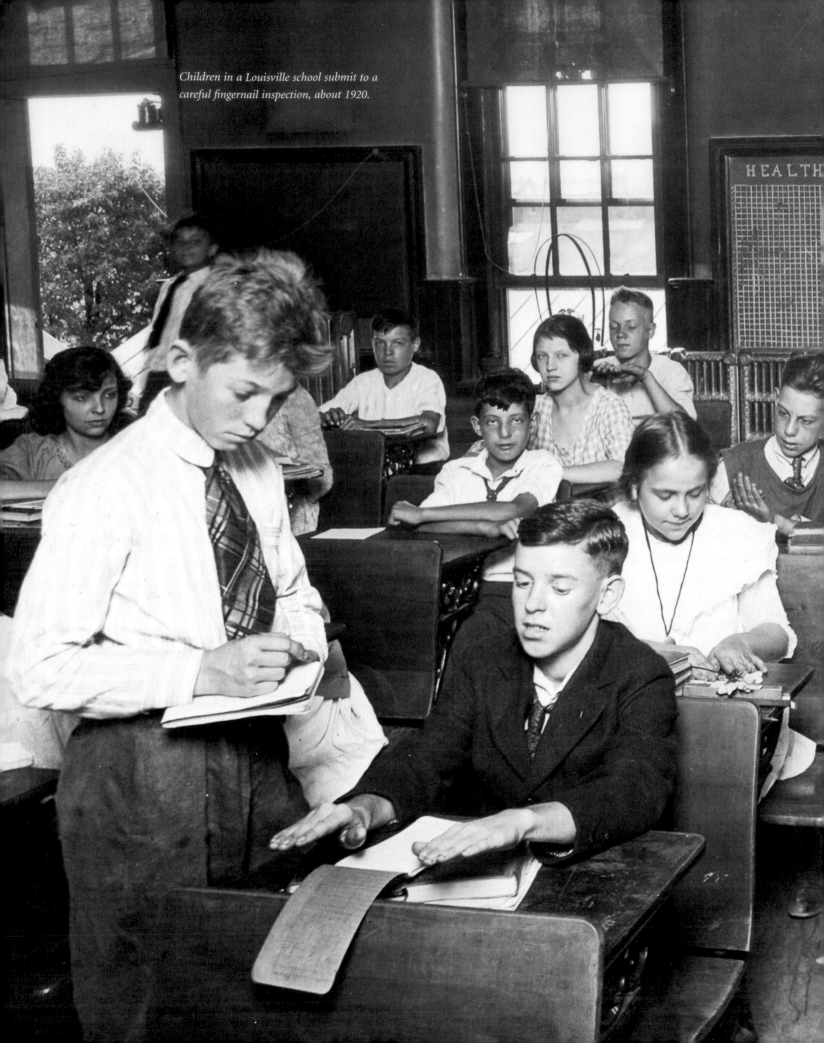

Children in a Louisville school submit to a careful fingernail inspection, about 1920.

Motorcycle cops flagged speeders, chased gangsters and escorted notables. These men, attired in varied uniforms, were photographed near San Diego.

Chicago police arrest bathers for indecent exposure, 1922.

Children participate in a Harlem fashion contest, about 1928.

GREEN'S
EMPLOYMEN
AGENCY
ROOM S
COLORED
HELP
A SPECIALT

HOURS
7.30
SATUR

The Quest for Normalcy

On the crisp, clear morning of March 4, 1921, in Washington, D.C., a parade of stately touring cars drove along Pennsylvania Avenue from the White House to the Capitol building. At the procession's head, in the rear seat of a Pierce-Arrow, sat two men in top hats and velvet-collared chesterfields *(below, left)*: Woodrow Wilson, the outgoing President of the United States, and his successor, Warren Gamaliel Harding. In the inaugural ceremony that was about to take place, the country was changing not only its chief executive, but also its mood, its outlook and its aspirations.

No two leaders could have been less alike. Wilson, prim and scholarly-looking, was a man whose era had passed. In the name of idealism, he had led America through a devastating war in Europe. In peacetime he had crusaded for reform at home and had admonished the nation to take up new responsibilities of world leadership. But Americans had grown tired of responsibilities and crusades. In the election of 1920 the country rejected Wilson's policies, leaving him embittered and broken, his health and his dreams shattered.

An Era of Uncertainty: The abandonment of Wilson reflected a change in the nation's basic attitudes. The promised millennium of world peace and democracy still had not arrived. After the slaughter and the privations of the war, people felt that their efforts had not really been worth it. Other moral certainties of earlier years also were coming under attack. Disturbing notions, such as the sexual theories of Sigmund Freud and the barely comprehensible discoveries of Albert Einstein, were eroding the sanctity of family life and challenging man's preeminence in the scheme of things. With its old values going sour, the nation was self-conscious and unsure of itself. America seemed suspended between the innocence and security of childhood and the wisdom and poise of maturity.

Many Americans reacted to the unsettling new elements of the era by affecting a kind of romantic cynicism. Like the youthful F. Scott Fitzgerald, they professed "to find all Gods dead, all wars fought, all

The old President (left) rides with the new to the 1921 inauguration.

> "America's present need is not heroics but healing; not nostrums but normalcy; not revolution but restoration; not surgery but serenity."

Warren G. Harding, 1920

faiths in man shaken." Others simply refused to worry themselves about anything but their own business; almost everybody agreed that the problems of the world were too confusing, and had best be ignored.

Passive Presidency: The man America turned to at the start of the decade seemed to offer a happy escape from the rigors of problem solving. Like the nation that elected him, he was something of an adolescent. Warren Harding never allowed the problems of high office to mar his congenial good humor. "The most notable quality of Harding was the sweetness of his nature," wrote a contemporary. "He gave out love." That Harding was not a particularly able man apparently bothered no one. The only fault anyone seemed to find with him was a fondness for what he called "bloviating," or windy speechmaking—a practice described by William Gibbs McAdoo, a former Secretary of the Treasury, as giving "the impression of an army of pompous phrases moving over the landscape in search of an idea." In the Presidential car on that March morning in 1921, Harding strained to make conversation with the sick man next to him. He told Wilson about his fondness for pet animals. He said that some day he would like to own a pet elephant. Wilson, in a thin attempt at humor, said he hoped the elephant would not be a white one.

For Harding the Presidency was just that. The new President suffered from a vital flaw: he refused to face responsibility. One of the problems that eluded his attention was the fact that his cronies were systematically robbing the public till. During his Presidency one close friend in a government post was revealed to be involved in graft, and two others committed suicide to escape prosecution. His Secretary of the Interior, Albert Fall, was implicated in an oil scandal, and rumors were circulating about his Attorney General, Harry Daugherty, who had mysteriously banked $75,000 while he was earning a salary of only $12,000. Shaken by these betrayals, Harding died in office on August 2, 1923, of a heart attack.

Despite all this, Harding's policy of governmental inactivity had been popular, and his successor, Calvin Coolidge, tried to carry it a step farther. To make sure he did nothing to rock the boat, Coolidge spent from two to four hours of every working day taking a nap.

In the freewheeling mood of the decade, strong government seemed not only boring, but also unnecessary. The nation's troubles,

In his wildly popular cover illustrations, artist John Held Jr. affectionately satirized the youthful excesses of the age, including a flapper's fondness for dance (top) and her newfound pleasure in driving a car (above).

people felt, were somehow solving themselves, without official interference. Though business had slumped a bit at the beginning of the decade, the economy soon began to boom. Overblown rumors of a Communist conspiracy had aroused fears just after the war; but the last incident of any importance had been in September 1920, when an anarchist bomb had exploded on Wall Street opposite the plutocratic Morgan bank.

Search for Sensation: Instead of problems, Americans in the '20s craved excitement. Almost anything, no matter how trivial or preposterous, seemed to give it to them—a gory murder in the tabloids, a world championship boxing match, a royal visit. In 1924, when Britain's young Prince of Wales made a pleasure jaunt to the United States, the nation went wild with excitement. Similar enthusiasm was lavished on Queen Marie of Romania when she toured the country in 1926, accompanied by a retinue of press agents. When a lanky, soft-spoken youth named Charles Lindbergh made the first solo airplane flight nonstop from New York to Paris in 1927, America pulled out the stops. As he was escorted up Broadway, jubilant crowds showered the returning hero with 1,800 tons of shredded paper.

The Prince of Wales gazes at Gotham's towers during his 1924 visit.

Hero Charles A. Lindbergh is welcomed to Broadway by ticker tape.

A spirit of frivolity seized the country. Women began cutting their hair at ear level and hemming their dresses to knee level. Otherwise respectable citizens began dancing the Charleston, carrying hip flasks and visiting speakeasies. H. L. Mencken, caustic critic of contemporary whims and vagaries, was once asked why, if he found so much to complain about in America, he bothered to live there. "Why do men go to zoos?" he replied.

The unrestrained hedonism of the decade fed on its own momentum. The Prohibition amendment that became law in 1920 had turned the simple pleasure of sipping a tot of whiskey into a federal offense—and many Americans began regularly and unremorsefully to violate the law. While many were seeking escape from responsibility through bathtub gin, others went to the movies. Here was a world where fantasy and flamboyance galloped unchecked. Settings became ever more extravagant, costumes more exotic, sex more emphatic. By the time Hollywood had supplemented sex with the additional inducement of sound, movies had become a way of life for most of America. The first talkie arrived in 1927 in the form of a film called *The Jazz Singer*, starring Al Jolson in blackface. By 1930 the silents had flickered out, and the talkies were pulling in 90 million viewers a week.

The decade also offered escape in the theater. While some playwrights, such as Eugene O'Neill, were writing intense dramas of deep psychological import, most of the nation's theatergoers preferred lighter fare. Comedy, or a kind of smiling-through-the-tears sentimentality, remained the order of the day. One Broadway show, a hearts-and-flowers romance between a Jewish boy and an Irish colleen, was so unabashedly mawkish that critics hated it and audiences professed to be embarrassed by it. Yet *Abie's Irish Rose* ran for 2,327 performances over a period of five years and five months, setting a record for theatrical longevity.

Mobsters' bodies sprawl in a garage on February 14, 1925 (page 126).

Booming Economy: Buoying up the pleasures and frivolities of the '20s was the most spectacular economic boom the country had ever seen. If some Americans felt disillusioned with politics or religion, they could find solace in a new faith based on the omnipotence of the dollar. Materialism flourished like an evangelical cult as the country placed its faith in the supreme importance of automobiles and washing machines. If not everyone was growing rich, people felt that the chances of becoming rich were getting better every day. During the period from 1921 to 1929, the gross national product soared from $74 billion to $104.4 billion. The buying power of wages for a skilled laborer swelled 50 percent from 1913 to 1927. Bricklayers' wives began to spruce up their wardrobes with silk stockings and white gloves. Their husbands began riding about in Niagara Blue roadsters or Arabian Sand phaetons.

Beneath all the self-conscious gaiety of the '20s, serious problems lurked; life and its concerns did not go away just because people were not paying attention. The prosperity and excitement that millions of Americans enjoyed eluded millions of others. Many of the country's people—especially in rural areas—had never tasted a drop of bathtub gin, never played mah-jongg, never heard of Freud, knew of jazz babies and flappers only through the movies, read their Bible faithfully and

Introducing talkies in 1927, Al Jolson vocalizes in The Jazz Singer.

Crowds gather after a bomb blasted Wall Street in 1920, killing 30.

Nicola Sacco (left) and Bartolomeo Vanzetti await their trial in 1920.

believed every word the Gospel said. In thousands of small communities, from the cotton fields of the South to the wheat-covered plains of the Middle West, life went on as usual.

Gathering Storm: In some places it was worse than usual. Large sections of the economy had failed to recover from the "temporary" economic downturn of 1920-1921. The index of farm prices, which had stood at 205 at the beginning of 1920, had plummeted to 116 a year later and by 1927 had only returned to 131. Western lumbermen, New England textile workers and coal miners in Pennsylvania and West Virginia suffered nearly as badly. Worst of all was the plight of the black sharecropper in the South, who lived in virtual economic slavery. He gave up to 75 per-cent of all the cotton or tobacco he raised to his white landlord. His income from the remainder amounted to less than $350 a year. On top of everything else, black citizens suffered from a resurgence of racial hatred. During the first half of the decade there was a rebirth of the Ku Klux Klan, a white supremacist organization dating from Reconstruc-tion days; Klan membership swelled to four million by 1924.

Amid the general indifference of the decade, only a few instances of social injustice managed to ruffle the conscience of the nation—or, more accurately, of a small but vocal part of the nation. The chief *cause célèbre* was the Sacco-Vanzetti case. On May 5, 1920, two professed anarchists named Nicola Sacco and Bartolomeo Vanzetti were arrested on charges that they had killed two men in a payroll robbery at South Braintree, Massachusetts. Both men were immigrants, neither could speak English very well and both had avoided the World War I draft on ideological grounds. To some Americans the evidence against Sacco and Vanzetti seemed inconclusive, and many were convinced that the two men were the victims of raw prejudice because they were foreign-ers, radicals and draft dodgers. Nevertheless, after seven years of litiga-tion and uproar the men were executed.

In short, serious matters persisted in intruding on the fun and frolic of the '20s. Even among the most frivolous there was an air of despera-tion. "What most distinguishes the generation who have approached

maturity since the debacle of idealism at the end of the War," said Walter Lippmann, "is not their rebellion against the religion and the moral code of their parents, but their disillusionment with their own rebellion. It is common for young men and women to rebel, but that they should rebel sadly and without faith in their rebellion, that they should distrust the new freedom no less than the old certainties—that is something of a novelty." Behind the bright surface of the '20s, its carnival of public events, the glitter of its prosperity, its love of revelry, lay an abiding sense of futility. The axiom of the decade was "Eat, drink and be merry," but it had its corollary: "For tomorrow we die."

On October 24, 1929, came the event that (though few realized it then) brought the decade to a close. On that day the stock market, which had been wavering for weeks, suddenly plunged. It was only the beginning *(page 90)*. The Great Depression had begun; in the rigors of this disaster, the strength of America would be sorely tried.

Flaming Youth

★

Boys and girls on Long Island brazenly puff on cigarettes.

An Age of Sheiks and Shebas

The '20s were an exciting—and perhaps a frightening—time to be young. It was the era of the First Youth Rebellion. Once boys had tried to be paragons of gallantry, industry and idealism; girls had aspired to seem modest and maidenly. Now all that had changed. "The uncertainties of 1919 were over," F. Scott Fitzgerald wrote. "America was going on the greatest, gaudiest spree in history."

In a refrain that would be heard again and again in

The advent of Prohibition made clandestine drinking an appealing game; women took up the sport alongside men. They also took up smoking; sales of cigarettes doubled during the decade.

Morals were undergoing a revolution. More and more college-age boys owned automobiles—and were parking them on dark roads to "neck" with their dates. Suddenly Freud's name was on everyone's lips. One writer complained: "Today, let some ingénue venture, 'I had the queerest dream—' and all at once we see a crowd, a host of parlor analysts. The obliging interpreters listen—though this is hardly necessary—look wise, and at the end exclaim 'Aha! That means *sex!* You have a sex-complex!'"

Inevitably, the daring clothes, the scandalous dances

"They're all desperadoes, these kids, all of them with any life in their veins; the girls as well as the boys; maybe more than the boys."

—Flaming Youth by Warner Fabian

---

later generations, John F. Carter Jr. wrote in the *Atlantic Monthly*: "I would like to observe that the older generation had certainly pretty well ruined this world before passing it on to us. They give us this Thing, knocked to pieces, leaky, red-hot, threatening to blow up; and then they are surprised that we don't accept it with the same enthusiasm with which they received it."

The new questioning of their elders' authority, combined with the relative affluence of the decade, spawned a breed of youngsters who claimed to be hard-boiled, heavy-drinking and daring—and sometimes were. The girls in particular seemed to have changed. Skirts were shorter than ever before. Cloche hats, silk stockings, fake jewelry, bobbed hair replaced the osprey plumes, hobble skirts and flowing tresses of yesteryear.

and sensual jazz, the late-night parties and cynical opinions of the young drew the wrath of many members of the older generation. "The situation," declared a Southern Baptist publication, "causes grave concern on the part of all who have the ideals at heart of purity and home life and the stability of our American civilization."

But America's young people didn't care. They went right on in their heedless, happy way, adopting the outrageous fashions shown on the following pages, and singing, "In the mean time, in between time, ain't we got fun?"

Poised and chic, the epitome of the sophisticated flapper, Suzette Dewey, daughter of the Assistant Secretary of the Treasury, steps out of her roadster.

Comic Joe E. Lewis displays golf hose, knickers and bow tie.

Submitting stoically to a men's barber, a girl has her hair bobbed.

Two women model winter fashion: open galoshes and cloche hats.

An amateur artist decorates a flapper's full-length rain slicker.

Patent-leather hair, center-parted, provides the movie-hero look.

A young man in Los Angeles shows off his white "Oxford bags."

A raccoon coat and peekaboo hat are de rigeur for the lady of fashion.

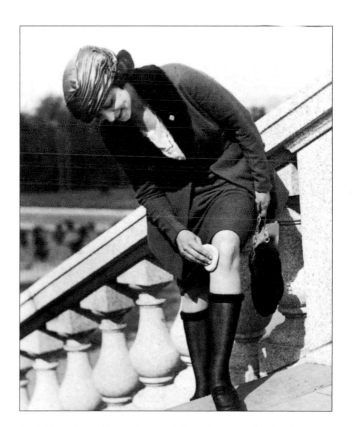

A girl in a short skirt and turned-down hose powders her knees.

The Jazz Age Glossary

The exuberant '20s were extraordinarily fertile years for language in America; dozens of new words and expressions sprang into existence. Much of the new verbiage was scornful of established ways; no less than half a dozen of the terms are roughly synonymous words meaning "nonsense." A partial list of terms that were coined or popularized in the decade appears below.

All wet—*wrong; arguing a mistaken notion or belief.*

Applesauce—*a term of derogation; nonsense; same as baloney, bunk, banana oil, hokum and horsefeathers.*

Baloney—*nonsense; same as applesauce, etc.*

Banana oil—*nonsense; same as above.*

Bee's knees—*a superb person or thing.*

Belly laugh—*a loud, uninhibited laugh.*

Berries—*anything wonderful; similar to bee's knees.*

Bible belt—*an area in the South or south Midwest where Fundamentalist religion prevails (coined by H. L. Mencken).*

Dumb Dora

Big cheese—*an important person.*

Blind date—*a date with an unknown person of the opposite sex, usually arranged by a mutual friend.*

Bronx cheer—*a loud derisive noise from an audience (coined by the humorist Bugs Baer, who credited Bronx rooters at athletic events with inventing this mode of expression).*

Bull session—*an informal group discussion.*

Bump off—*to murder.*

Bunk—*nonsense; same as applesauce, etc. (a shortened form of "bunkum," which is also*

Big Cheese

spelled "buncombe," from the name of a North Carolina county whose representative in Congress in 1820 explained the irrelevance of a speech he was making by saying that he was "talking to Buncombe").

Cake-eater—*a ladies' man.*

Carry a torch—*to suffer from unrequited love.*

Cat's meow—*anything wonderful; similar to bee's knees, berries.*

Cheaters—*eyeglasses.*

Copacetic—*excellent.*

Crush—*an infatuation with a person of the opposite sex.*

Darb—*an excellent person or thing.*

Dogs—*human feet.*

Drugstore cowboy—*a fashionably dressed idler who hangs around public places trying to pick up girls.*

Dumb Dora—*a stupid girl.*

Fall guy—*a scapegoat.*

Flapper—*a typical young girl of the '20s, usually with bobbed hair, short skirts and rolled stockings.*

Flat tire—*a dull, boring person.*

Frame—*to cause a person's arrest by giving false evidence.*

Gam—*a girl's leg (from French dialect "gambe").*

Gatecrasher—*a person who attends a party without an invitation, or a show without paying admission.*

Giggle water—*an alcoholic drink.*

Gin mill—*a speakeasy.*

Gold digger—*a woman who uses feminine charm to extract money from a man.*

Goofy—*silly.*

Gyp—*to cheat (from "gypsy").*

Hard-boiled—*tough; without sentiment.*

Heebie-jeebies—*the jitters.*

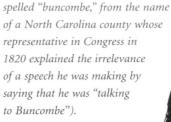
Drugstore Cowboy

Flapper

Jalopy

Hep—*wise.*

High-hat—*to snub.*

Hokum—*nonsense; same as applesauce, etc.*

Hooch—*bootleg liquor (from "Hoochinoo," a tribe of Alaskan Indians who made distilled liquor).*

Hoofer—*chorus girl.*

Horsefeathers—*nonsense; same as applesauce, etc.*

Hotsy-totsy—*pleasing.*

Jake—*okay (most commonly used in the phrase "Everything's jake").*

Jalopy—*an old car.*

Keen—*attractive; appealing.*

Kiddo—*a familiar form of address.*

Kisser—*the mouth.*

Line—*insincere flattery.*

Lounge lizard—*a ladies' man; same as cake-eater.*

Lousy—*bad; contemptible.*

Main drag—*the most important street in a town or city.*

Neck—*to caress intimately.*

Nerts (Nuts)—*an interjection expressing the speaker's disgust.*

Ossified—*drunk.*

Peppy—*full of vitality.*

Pet—*same as neck.*

Pinch—*to arrest.*

Pushover—*a person or thing easily overcome.*

Necking

Raspberry—*same as Bronx cheer.*

Ritzy—*elegant (from "Ritz," the Paris hotel).*

Real McCoy, the—*the genuine article (the derivation is in dispute; it comes either from a Scottish clan leader named MacKay; a boxer named Kid McCoy, who had a rival with the same name, or a bootlegger named McCoy who did not adulterate his liquor).*

Run-around—*deceptive or delaying action, especially in response to a request.*

Scram—*to leave hurriedly (from "scramble").*

Screwy—*crazy; eccentric.*

Sex appeal—*physical attractiveness to members of the opposite sex.*

Sheik and Sheba

Sheba—*a young woman with sex appeal.*

Sheik—*a young man with sex appeal.*

Smeller—*the nose.*

Sob sister—*a woman reporter who leans toward sentimentality in the treatment of her subject matter.*

Speakeasy—*a saloon or bar selling bootleg whiskey.*

Spifflicated—*drunk.*

Spiffy—*having an elegantly fashionable appearance.*

Struggle buggy—*a car (from its use as a place in which boys tried to seduce girls).*

Stuck on—*having a crush on.*

Swanky—*ritzy.*

Swell—*marvelous.*

Torpedo—*a hired gunman.*

Upchuck—*to vomit.*

Whoopee—*boisterous, convivial fun.*

Hooch

That Barbaric Music

Social dancing," wrote a female evangelist in the Portland *Oregonian*, "is the first and easiest step toward hell. The modern dance cheapens womanhood. The first time a girl allows a man to swing her around the dance floor her instinct tells her she has lost something she should have treasured." What she usually lost was her corset. Most "nice" girls were forced by their mothers to wear foundation garments, but the flappers hated them; they discouraged men and made it uncomfortable to do dances like the black bottom, the shimmy and the Charleston. Therefore, as soon as girls arrived at parties they rushed into the ladies' room and "parked their girdles."

Once liberated, the girls were free to indulge in the slow fox trots of the day or to break loose during the faster, jazzier numbers. Jazz songs seemed somehow uncivilized—and therefore desirable—to the young. As one young man commented: "Our music is distinctly barbaric, our girls are distinctly *not* a mixture of arbutus and barbed-wire. After all, we have just discovered that we are still very near to the Stone Age." Whether savage or suggestive or just silly, the song lyrics captured the high spirits of the decade, as the excerpts below demonstrate.

Runnin' wild, lost control
Runnin' wild, mighty bold
Feelin' gay, reckless too.

I'm the sheik of Araby,
Your love belongs to me.
At night when you're asleep,
Into your tent I'll creep.

If you knew Susie like I know Susie,
Oh! Oh! Oh! what a girl!
We went riding, She didn't balk
Back from Yonkers,
I'm the one that had to walk!

Young flappers competing in the Charleston Endurance Contest at New York's Parody Club are given much needed sustenance in mid-step by helpful band members.

Hollywood Fans the Flames

I n the '20s flaming youth learned to burn more brightly by imitating the antics of the stars in Hollywood movies. Girls copied the romantic techniques of great vamps like Theda Bara, studied sex appeal from Clara Bow *(below)* and learned the art of smiling winsomely from Mary Pickford.

One of the most popular screen flappers was Joan Crawford, who drew huge crowds in 1928 to her film about decadent youth, *Our Dancing Daughters.* Millions of girls watched breathlessly as Crawford drank, kissed and, best of all, showed how to cross and uncross one's hands on one's knees while doing the Charleston. The film was so successful that she made a sequel, *Our Modern Maidens.* In this one Crawford played a married woman who flirts with a bachelor, gets divorced and—scandalous!—lives happily ever after.

What Crawford did for the girls, Rudolph Valentino did for the boys. Following his lead, American men learned

Clara Bow, languishing in a negligee, radiates "It," a quality she confusedly thought described the ability to give undivided attention in conversation.

to tango, and to pop their eyes and bare their teeth while making love. Advertising copywriters did their part, too; one movie ad promised "brilliant men, beautiful jazz babies, champagne baths, midnight revels, petting parties in the purple dawn, all ending in one terrific smashing climax that makes you gasp." The films really were not quite that exciting, but they didn't have to be; they sparked the nation's youngsters anyhow. "Those pictures with hot lovemaking in them," one 16-year-old girl told a writer, "they make girls and boys sitting together want to get up and walk out, go off somewhere, you know."

If there was any one person who made the kids get

up and walk out it was Clara Bow, who turned the innocent little pronoun "It" into the most suggestive word in the language. Elinor Glyn, a popular author of love stories, had written a novel called *It*. In Madame Glyn's book, "It" was not a thing; it was a quality (always capitalized). She defined it this way: "To have 'It,' the fortunate possessor must have that strange magnetism which attracts both sexes. There must be physical attraction, but beauty is unnecessary."

When Madame Glyn came to Hollywood to find a girl who possessed "It," she elected Clara Bow, a tiny starlet with bee-stung lips, flat chest, big eyes and dimpled knees. Soon the "It" girl was one of the leading five box-office draws in Hollywood.

The story of her rise to stardom was like something invented by a press agent. She had been born very poor in Brooklyn. Scorned by other girls because of her shabby clothes, she turned to boys. When she was 16 she entered a beauty contest, won first prize and was whisked off to Hollywood for a bit part. Her performance ended up on the cutting-room floor, however, and her psychotic mother was so horrified at the prospect of her daughter becoming an actress that she tried to stab Clara. But the girl persevered, soon won recognition in several films and then, when she was 21, was dubbed the "It" girl.

Her off-screen life also made good copy. Living in a modest bungalow and dressing casually (she wore pants before most other women dared), Clara apparently drove men mad with desire. A Yale football player slashed his wrists after she jilted him; he survived to tell a court during a sanity hearing that Clara had kissed him so passionately on one occasion that his lips had been bruised for two days. She bathed in perfume and refused to hire a chauffeur because none would drive fast enough. By the end of the decade, her luck was running out. After the stock-market crash, people were bored by flappers; worse, the advent of talkies revealed that Clara had a thick Brooklyn accent. For a few brief years, however, Hollywood's "It" girl lived up to her billing as "The Hottest Jazz Baby in Films."

F. Scott Fitzgerald studies one of his books. During the '20s he turned out three widely read novels; best known was This Side of Paradise.

The Creator of an Era

Much of the credit—or the blame—for the flapper era must be laid on the shoulders of F. Scott Fitzgerald. An exceptionally handsome and talented young man, Fitzgerald became famous overnight in 1920 upon the publication of his first novel, *This Side of Paradise*. Fitzgerald was only 24, and he was one of the first writers to draw attention to the new postwar sophistication and to such phenomena as youthful love affairs and "petting parties." The book was a huge success and, in the words of a fellow writer, Fitzgerald became "a kind of king of our American youth." If he was king, the queen was his beautiful, witty and unstable wife, Zelda. The royal couple became almost as well known for their madcap antics as for his writing. They rode on the hoods of taxis down Fifth Avenue, disrupted plays by laughing during the sad parts and weeping noisily over the jokes, and entertained lavishly at drunken parties. To foot the bills for their extravagant capers, Fitzgerald wrote scores of short stories for the slick magazines; both the stories and his novels record—and partly served to create—the period. These are excerpts.

"At eighteen our convictions are hills from which we look; at forty-five they are caves in which we hide."

F. Scott Fitzgerald, "Bernice Bobs Her Hair"

None of the Victorian mothers—and most of the mothers were Victorian—had any idea how casually their daughters were accustomed to be kissed. Amory saw girls doing things that even in his memory would have been impossible; eating three-o'clock, after-dance suppers in impossible cafés, talking of every side of life with an air half of earnestness, half of mockery, yet with a furtive excitement that Amory considered stood for a real moral let-down. But he never realized how widespread it was until he saw the cities between New York and Chicago as one vast juvenile intrigue.
–*This Side of Paradise*

People over forty can seldom be permanently convinced of anything. At eighteen our convictions are hills from which we look; at forty-five they are caves in which we hide.
–"Bernice Bobs Her Hair"

The restlessness approached hysteria. The parties were bigger. The pace was faster, the shows were broader, the buildings were higher, the morals were looser, and the liquor was cheaper; but all these benefits did not really minister to much delight. Young people wore out early—they were hard and languid at twenty-one. Most of my friends drank too much—the more they were in tune to the times the more they drank. The city was bloated, glutted, stupid with cake and circuses, and a new expression "Oh yeah?" summed up all the enthusiasm evoked by the announcement of the last super-skyscrapers.
–Commentary on New York, 1926.

He (After due consideration): This is a frightful thing to ask.
She (Knowing what's coming): After five minutes.
He: But will you—kiss me? Or are you afraid?
She: I'm never afraid—but your reasons are so poor.
He: Rosalind, I really want to kiss you.
She: So do I. (They kiss—definitely and thoroughly.)
He (After a breathless second): Well, is your curiosity satisfied?
She: Is yours?
He: No, it's only aroused. (He looks it.)
She (Dreamily): I've kissed dozens of men. I suppose I'll kiss dozens more.
–*This Side of Paradise*

Massed bombers dedicate the new Hollywood airport in 1930.

Flight

★

HUMANITY TAKES TO THE AIR

A Suddenly Smaller World

For American airmen, the early 1920s were years of frustration. During the war, many of them had known adulation; in particular, the folks back home had avidly followed the exploits of the pursuit pilots, whose man-to-man dogfights had supplied a touch of personal combat amid the mechanized slaughter of trench warfare. Now most Americans had reverted to their old

from Los Angeles to Reno, renowned for quickie divorces; Turner's route became known as the "Alimony Special." After this venture folded, Turner convinced an oil company whose trademark was a lion that it could get enormous publicity if it hired him to fly around the country with a lion cub as his passenger. The lion liked to fly, but the Humane Society insisted that Turner strap a parachute on the beast. Luckily, the cub never had to jump.

That was more than could be said about the pilots who worked for the Post Office Department's fledgling airmail service. Flying without instruments in all kinds of weather, many of them died when their planes iced up or hit mountainsides, but a good number were saved by

> "The airplane has now advanced to the stage where the demands of commerce are sufficient to warrant the building of planes without regard to military usefulness. Undoubtedly in a few years the United States will be covered with a network of passenger, mail and express lines."
>
> Charles A. Lindbergh, *We,* 1927

conviction that if God had wanted men to fly, He would have given them wings. Some fliers turned to other ways of making a living: Eddie Rickenbacker, America's Ace of Aces, sold autos. But there was a small group of men who doggedly stuck to the air; they soon found themselves engaged in a strange variety of airborne activities.

Ben O. Howard, pilot turned airplane designer, found a lucrative market in building planes for bootleggers, who needed the aircraft to smuggle illegal liquor across the Canadian or Mexican borders. Howard also flew the contraband cargoes himself—and got used to being shot at by moonshiners who thought they were being hunted from the air by revenue agents. Famed instructor and pilot Casey Jones sped urgent news photos cross-country. Another pilot, Roscoe Turner, set up an airline that ran

their parachutes. A tall, slender young airmail pilot named Charles A. Lindbergh bailed out four times without ever losing faith in aviation. In 1927 Lindbergh took off from Roosevelt Field, Long Island, in a tiny plane, and headed out over the ocean, bound for Europe. Some 33½ hours later he landed in Paris—and was stunned by the hysterical acclaim that greeted him. It was a justified tribute, for Lindbergh's exploit, the first nonstop solo transatlantic flight, was the transcendentally dramatic event which proved that the age of air transportation had truly begun. With this flight, the world was suddenly smaller.

Lindbergh stands beside The Spirit of St. Louis. He identified himself with his plane so closely that he used the term "we" in telling of their flight.

Ormer Locklear, the first to transfer from one moving plane to another, here adds a refinement by doing it head first. He later died in a filmed stunt crash.

"Your Money Back..."

Moving across the country with the seasons, keeping their aging planes in the air with ingenuity and baling wire, landing in any level pasture, the barnstorming pilots of the 1920s gave at least 10 million Americans their first introduction to flying, at five dollars per five-minute joy ride. Most of them flew Jennies—war surplus JN-4D trainers, thousands of which had been completed too late for the war and could now be had for as little as $300 each.

To get customers out to the field, the barnstormers learned showmanship. At first they merely buzzed low over a town while stunt men walked out on the lower wing. Then, as competition grew stiffer, the stunters became more imaginative: they stood on the upper wing, dangled from the lower wing, parachuted to earth. Once when business was slow, stunt man Wesley May crouched on the top wing of a plane with a can of gasoline strapped to his back, while another plane flew alongside, wingtip-to-wingtip. Then May stepped across to the other plane, walked the length of its wing, and poured the fuel into its tank.

Aerial clowns were also good for business. "Wild Bill" Kopia's act was a favorite. Dressed as a bosomy operatic soprano, he would buy a ticket and climb into the passenger cockpit of a Jenny whose propeller was idly ticking over. Suddenly the pilot would jump out, presumably to get something he'd forgotten, and at that moment the Jenny would lurch forward with the apparently terrified "soprano" yelling for help. Nearing the boundary fence, the Jenny would abruptly climb into the air and then Wild Bill would put on a superb demonstration of aerobatics, to the delight and astonishment of the crowd.

The financial returns for taking these risks were skimpy. Dick Depew, one of the barnstormers, once remarked solemnly that "the most dangerous thing about flying is the risk of starving to death." It was certainly true that barnstorming was safer than it looked, for the pilots were among the most skilled airmen of their time. "All rides are guaranteed to get you back in one piece," one pitchman used to cry. "Your money back if you get killed!"

One ever-popular ploy while airborne was to attempt some sporting maneuver such as the golf swing taken by stunt man Al Wilson (above) at 3,000 feet.

Carrying the Mail

Scheduled airmail had an inauspicious beginning. On the very first flight, a Washington–New York run, the plane started to take off, then stopped; someone had forgotten to fill the fuel tank. The mail finally got off the ground, but the pilot became lost and made a forced landing in Maryland. The flight never did get to New York.

In the years that followed, the mail got through with increasing regularity, in spite of ill-equipped planes and unreliable weather reports. The death toll was apalling: 31 of the first 40 pilots to fly the mail from New York to Chicago were killed in crashes.

Nonetheless, the fliers took pride in getting the mail through, and on time. On February 22, 1921, pilot Jack Knight landed in Omaha after a 248-mile flight from North Platte, Nebraska, one leg of a history-making trip—the first transcontinental day-and-night delivery (previously the planes had landed at nightfall). Knight was looking forward to a long sleep when the field manager informed him that no pilot was available for the next leg, a 424-mile jaunt to Chicago.

Uppermost in the minds of both men was the knowledge that Congress would be voting the next day on the mail appropriation; both realized that their performance could dramatically affect the outcome of that vote. Knight climbed back into the plane and took off on the unfamiliar route. He arrived at his refueling stop, Iowa City, in heavy snow, then flew through thick fog to a triumphant landing in Chicago. Two other pilots completed the journey to New York; total elapsed time across the continent had been 33 hours 20 minutes—an incredible record for the period. Congress passed the bill. Soon better planes came into service, and air-postage rates, reflecting the growing dependability of the mail, dropped from 24 cents to 10 cents a half ounce. A stamp was issued showing the rate change (above)—a signal to mail pilots that the service had finally come of age.

A mail pilot, bundled up, prepares to board his Boeing. This plane had a passenger compartment; travelers no longer had to hold the mail on their laps.

AIR RAIL AIR RAIL

COAST TO COAST IN 48 HOURS

(Daily Through service effective from New York July 7—from Port Columbus July 8, 1929)

The schedule and meal arrangements for the through route between New York, N. Y. and Los Angeles, Cal., and San Francisco, Cal., are given below. Passengers will be ticketed from Pittsburgh, Cleveland or any station on the Pennsylvania Railroad on convenient connecting train service to and from Columbus. Tickets will be also sold from all stations for any combination of rail and air service included in the through route.

WESTBOUND

Pennsylvania Railroad
THE AIRWAY LIMITED
Eastern Time

Lv. New York (Penna. Sta.), N.Y.*	6.05 PM
Lv. North Philadelphia, Pa.	7.50 PM
Lv. Washington, D.C.	6.30 PM
Lv. Baltimore, Md.	7.30 PM
Ar. Port Columbus, O.†	7.55 AM

Transcont'l Air Transp. Inc.

	Central Time
Lv. Port Columbus, O.	8.15 AM
Ar. Indianapolis, Ind.	9.13 AM
Lv. Indianapolis, Ind.	9.28 AM
Ar. St. Louis, Mo.	12.03 PM
Lv. St. Louis, Mo.‡	12.18 PM
Ar. Kansas City, Mo.	2.47 PM
Lv. Kansas City, Mo.	3.02 PM
Ar. Wichita, Kansas	4.56 PM
Lv. Wichita, Kansas	5.11 PM
Ar. Airport, Okla. (Landing Field)§	6.24 PM
Transfer to Waynoka by Aero Car

Atch., Topeka & Santa Fe Ry.
Sleeping car ready for occupancy
at 8.00 P.M

	Central Time
	11.00 PM
Lv. Waynoka, Okla.	8.20 AM
Ar. Clovis, N. M.	
Transfer to Portair by Aero Car

Transcont'l Air Transp. Inc.
Mountain Time

Lv. Portair, N. M. Landing Field	8.10 AM
Ar. Albuquerque, N. M.	10.17 AM
Lv. Albuquerque, N. M.	10.52 AM
Ar. Winslow, Ariz.	1.12 PM
Lv. Winslow, Ariz.‡	1.27 PM
	Pacific Time
Ar. Kingman, Ariz.	2.51 PM
Lv. Kingman, Ariz.	2.46 PM
Ar. Los Angeles, Cal.	5.52 PM
(Grand Central Air Terminal, Glendale, Cal. Passengers will be transferred by Aero Car to and from the central section of Los Angeles.)

San Francisco passengers upon arrival at Los Angeles will be given the option of using overnight trains either from Los Angeles or Glendale, or they may remain overnight in Los Angeles and proceed by Maddux Airline plane morning service from Glendale Airport to San Francisco. Transfers will be provided by aero car between Glendale and the central section of Los Angeles. Tickets for whichever plan is selected by passenger will be furnished by the Transcontinental Air Transport, Inc.

EASTBOUND

Transcont'l Air Transp. Inc.
Pacific Time

	8.45 AM
Lv. Los Angeles, Cal (Grand Central Air Terminal, Glendale)	
Ar. Kingman, Ariz.	11.18 AM
Lv. Kingman, Ariz.‡	11.33 AM
	Mountain Time
	2.14 PM
Ar. Winslow, Ariz.	2.29 PM
Lv. Winslow, Ariz.	
Ar. Albuquerque, N. M.**	4.40 PM
Lv. Albuquerque, N. M.	5.10 PM
Ar. Portair, N. M. Landing Field	6.54 PM
Transfer to Clovis by Aero Car

Atch., Topeka & Santa Fe Ry.
Sleeping car ready for occupancy
at 9.00 P.M

	Central Time
	11.35 PM
Lv. Clovis, N. M.	8.10 AM
Ar. Waynoka, Okla.⊙	
Transfer to Airport by Aero Car

Transcont'l Air Transp. Inc.
Central Time

Lv. Airport, Okla. Landing Field	8.55 AM
Ar. Wichita, Kansas	9.55 AM
Lv. Wichita, Kansas	10.10 AM
Ar. Kansas City, Mo.	11.43 AM
Lv. Kansas City, Mo.‡	11.58 AM
Ar. St. Louis, Mo.	2.00 PM
Lv. St. Louis, Mo.	2.15 PM
Ar. Indianapolis, Ind.	4.22 PM
Lv. Indianapolis, Ind.	4.37 PM
	Eastern Time
Ar. Port Columbus, O.	7.13 PM

Pennsylvania Railroad
THE AMERICAN

Lv. Port Columbus, O.*	7.46 PM
Ar. North Philadelphia, Pa.	8.05 PM
Ar. New York (Penna. Sta.), N.Y.	9.50 AM
Ar. Baltimore, Md.	9.05 AM
Ar. Washington, D.C.	10.05 AM

From San Francisco passengers will be given the option of using overnight trains from San Francisco, arriving Glendale next morning, making direct connection with eastbound afternoon plane, arriving Grand Central Air Terminal, Glendale and will be transported by Aero car to the central section of Los Angeles. The next morning they will be transported by Aero car to the airport at Glendale.

*Dinner and breakfast on Pennsylvania Railroad Dining Car. †A new station stop (Port Columbus) seven (7) miles east of Columbus, O. ‡Luncheon on plane—Fred Harvey Service. §Transfer to Harvey House, Waynoka, Okla., where dinner will be served. ‖Breakfast at Harvey House, Santa Fe Station—**Dinner at Albuquerque, Airport—Fred Harvey Service. ⊙Breakfast at Harvey House

Apply to any Pennsylvania Railroad agent for full information as to fares, checking baggage, other schedules, etc.

PENNSYLVANIA RAILROAD

The announcement of combined air-rail service in 1929 (above) promised travelers a 36-hour saving over the fastest train. Dark blocks indicate night travel.

Profits from Passengers

After Lindbergh's flight to Paris, Americans took to the skies in increasing numbers. Watching air passenger figures quadruple in 1928, financiers decided that aviation might actually prove profitable. Securities were marketed, the infant airlines ordered big trimotor airplanes, and new airports were built to accommodate them.

But night travel was still considered too hazardous for passenger operations. The first coast-to-coast service was set up as a hybrid: the travelers flew by day, transferred to train at night; the entire trip took a solid, exhausting two days. The service was launched with enormous fanfare. The maiden journey departed from Los Angeles on July 8, 1929; eastbound, Lindbergh himself piloted the plane, which had been christened by screen star Mary Pickford. Enthusiasm for air travel was running high, but it was far from universal. The president of one airline admitted that he never flew in his company's planes when he could avoid it—and his wife flatly refused to fly at all.

Passengers board the Fokker with which Pan American began its international service in 1928. One-way fare, Key West to Havana, was $50.

A steward serves up a meal. At one point airlines used weighty crockery, designed to stay put in bumpy air. Airsick travelers got a lemon to suck.

This Ford Tri-motor boasted a steward and weightsaving wicker seats.

The ample costumes of the first stewardesses (left) combated cabin drafts.

Airline publicity photos stressed the luxury features of the new transport planes, such as this Fokker F-32 sleeping compartment with tapestried panels.

All That Jazz

★

BLACK AMERICA'S GIFT TO THE WORLD

Carroll Dickerson's band plays for a jazz floor show: Chicago, 1924.

> "Aw, play that thing,
> Mr. St. Cyr, lawd,
> you know you can do
> it! Everybody from
> New Orleans can really
> do that thing!"
>
> Louis Armstrong to the banjoist
> on "Gut Bucket Blues"

A modest canopy advertises Barron's Cabaret, a Harlem joint where jazz flourished. Duke Ellington got his start here in 1923.

The Syncopated Sound

This was the Jazz Age. The word took the country, or at least the country's youth, by storm. Dressmaking establishments advertised "jazz styles," poets wrote "jazz poetry." *The New York Times* reported in 1925 that Fifth Avenue matrons were vying hotly for black maids who could teach them how to do the Charleston.

Of course this behavior, and the music that prompted it, scandalized the guardians of the nation's morals. An upstate New York preacher fulminated: "Jazz may be analyzed as a combination of nervousness, lawlessness, primitive and savage animalism and lasciviousness." A Columbia University professor denounced it as the attempt of "a joyless industrial civilization to arouse its fatigue-poisoned minds and its drudgery-jaded bodies."

These cries of anathema affected the rage for jazz to about the same extent that Prohibition kept people from drinking. And jazz lovers soon had impressive reinforcements. Serious composers quickly grasped at elements in the new syncopated music. Darius Milhaud, a leading French modernist, wrote a ballet with jazz rhythms; Paul Hindemith weighed in with jazz piano suites; Maurice Ravel published a sonata with jazzy passages. America's great songwriter George Gershwin produced "serious" jazz compositions. These works sent the classical music critics into fits. Lawrence Gilman scathingly described Gershwin's *Rhapsody in Blue* as "trite," "feeble," "vapid," "fussy" and "futile."

But this "symphonic jazz" and most of the other music that passed for jazz in the '20s was not real jazz at all. The real music—like much great art through the centuries—was being produced in relative obscurity. It had moved upriver from New Orleans, its birthplace, but it was still heard mainly in black dance halls in Harlem and Chicago, and on records that were frankly labeled "race records" and sold only in African-American neighborhoods. And while the impresarios of ersatz jazz such as Paul Whiteman were making a quarter of a million dollars a year, the real jazzmen were often broke. The great Louis Armstrong had to play in dubious show bands such as Carroll Dickerson's *(pages 54-55)*, while Bix Beiderbecke wasted his glorious cornet tone tooting for third-rate dance bands. The real jazzmen traveled from date to date in rattletrap cars with the luggage tied on the roof. But the musicians were tough and so was the music and it survived the neglect of the age to which it gave the name and became America's one triumphant contribution to the world's music.

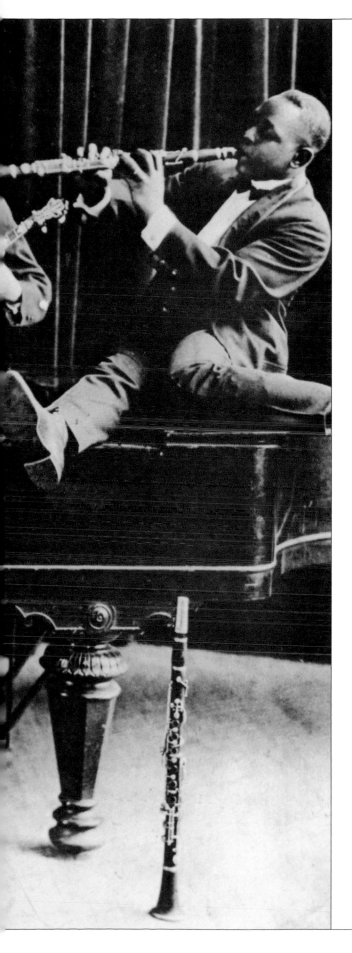

The King's Men

Who played the real stuff? The black residents of Chicago's South Side agreed that the best group of all in 1923 was King Oliver's Creole Jazz Band. The name "Creole" indicated its origin—the band was almost a Who's Who of the best musicians to come north from New Orleans. Johnny Dodds played the clarinet and his younger brother, called "Baby," was on drums. Joe Oliver, the cornet-playing leader, had long been acknowledged the Crescent City's top brass man and he had with him a new cornet-playing sensation from down home, a cheerful lad named Louis Armstrong. Joe and Louis could read each other's mind and when they did duet breaks, playing in perfect harmony with no rehearsal, the crowd at Chicago's Lincoln Gardens went wild, standing on tables and shouting. The band had, everyone agreed, "that great blue New Orleans sound," and Joe Oliver deserved his title of King.

Oliver was a powerfully built man of formidable girth. When he was about to blow something really hot he would say to the admirers grouped around the bandstand, "Now you'll get a chance to see Papa Joe's red underwear." And as he blew chorus after chorus his stiff shirt-front would pop and the red undershirt—he always wore one—would show through. "Papa Joe was a creator—always some little idea—and he exercised them beautifully," Armstrong recalled. "I'll never run out of ideas. All I have to do is think about Joe."

A great man, a great horn, a great band. The South Side of Chicago was something else. The Lincoln Gardens, as one patron remembered, was "dingy and needing several coats of paint. Ancient paper decorations and faded flowers hung dejectedly from unpainted walls and peeling columns." Like other South Side joints, it received visits from the toughest gangsters—members of Al Capone's mob. When fights or shooting erupted, it was the band's job to play as loudly as it could to cover up the noise of shattering bottles or gunfire. But despite the sordid surroundings and the violence, this is where true jazz first found an increasing audience and its own real voice.

In clownish poses, de rigueur for early jazz photos, King Oliver's Creole Jazz Band seems ready to blast the ears off pianist Lil Hardin.

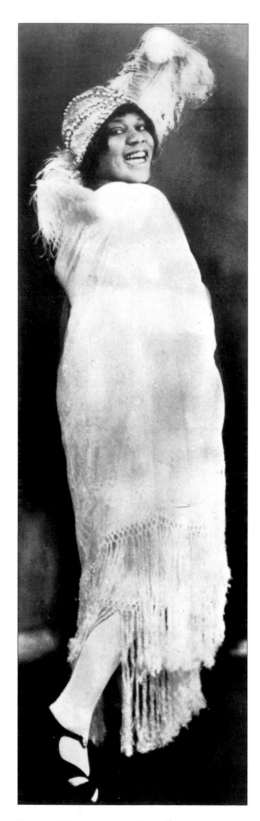

Feather, fringe and a bright smile:
Bessie Smith in 1925.

The Empress and Father Dip

A press agent made up the name "Empress of the Blues," but that is what Bessie Smith truly was. She sang with a power and an intensity of feeling unmatched by any other blues singer. Her records sold in the millions—although only in the South and the ghettos of the North. Her sound, as poet Langston Hughes said, "was too basic for the general public" and few white people in the '20s even knew her name. The records brought her a great deal of money. Unfortunately she spent it as fast as it came in. "A cat came up to her one day, wanted change for a thousand dollar bill—trying to see if she had it," Louis Armstrong recalled. "Bessie said, 'Yeah.' She just raised up the front of her dress and there was a carpenter's apron and she just pulled that change out of it. That was her bank."

The other towering figure in jazz as the '20s progressed was, of course, Armstrong himself—considered by many to have been, in his prime, the greatest jazz musician of them all. Born on July 4, 1900, he grew up in the toughest black neighborhood in New Orleans. At 12 he was put in a home for wayward boys for firing off a pistol on New Year's Eve. It was there, in the reformatory, that he learned the rudiments of playing the cornet. Released from the home, he hawked coal from a mule-drawn cart, delivered milk, worked on a junk wagon and stevedored on the docks. At night he took jobs playing his battered horn in rough cafes; during this period his principal income came from the tips prostitutes gave him to play the blues. It was a hard school, but Armstrong was good enough by 1920 to get jobs on Mississippi River excursion steamboats and, in 1922, to join Joe Oliver in Chicago. Before long he was overshadowing even the great King Oliver and, like Bessie, was famous in the black world. His great soaring solos and his magnificent trumpet tone remade jazz. As a boy, his large mouth and lips had given him the taunting nickname of Dippermouth. Now his fellow musicians, in awe and affection, gave him another nickname—Father Dip.

Louis Armstrong in the mid-'20s: boiled shirt, shy grin and gleaming trumpet, the
brilliantly toned horn he had exchanged for the cornet.

That Harlem Hotcha!

Suddenly Harlem was the thing. Its shows, as *Variety* proclaimed, had "pep, pulchritude, punch and presentation." And white people from downtown flocked northward to see them, especially the elaborate revues at Connie's Inn and the Cotton Club, both nightclubs catering mainly to white customers. Other clubs, of course, welcomed Harlem's own people and one dance hall, the Savoy, and one theater, the Lafayette, became hubs of night life.

The rage to visit Harlem and see black entertainment was triggered in 1921 when a superb musical show called *Shuffle Along*—written, produced and performed by blacks—was a smash hit on Broadway. It was followed within a four-year period by eight other black shows including *Liza*, *Runnin' Wild* and *Chocolate Dandies*. Broadway playgoers had never known music like this, or seen such dancing or heard such singing. They wanted

more, and the big Harlem clubs obliged with chorus lines, comedians, singers like Ethel Waters and marvelous dancers like Bill "Bojangles" Robinson. The clubs also provided the best big jazz bands of the period, notably Duke Ellington's and Fletcher Henderson's. But the bands were not, by and large, what the white folks went to see. They wanted, as *Variety* condescendingly put it, "high yeller gals" who could "uncork the meanest kind of cootching." They were, in effect, slumming and out for new thrills. Few could appreciate the music any more than they could see the real Harlem. But they were at least exposed to jazz, and their dollars helped it flourish. Harlem in the '20s developed no fewer than 11 nightspots *Variety* called "class white-trade night clubs," plus some 500 other jazz places. "The swarming, prosperous crowds bent on nocturnal diversion," as one observer put it, "found Harlem exotic and colorful. To them it seemed a citadel of jazz

and laughter where gaiety began after midnight."

Underneath the glitter, of course, all was not gaiety. This was, after all, Prohibition, and the owners of the Cotton Club included such unsavory bootleggers and gunmen as Owney Madden and George "Big Frenchy" De Mange. "Pineapples," as the people of the '20s called bombs, sometimes flew through the front windows of cabarets and blew out the back walls. But despite the violence, despite the segregation in the "class white-trade" places, despite the bad booze in the speakeasies, the idiom of Harlem crossed the continent and the oceans.

The influence of jazz, good and bad, began to spread. Its dissemination was aided by the phonograph record: dozens of companies vied to get on wax the newly famous black stars, along with their white imitators. Almost unnoticed amid all the cooch dancers and chorus lines, the great music was making its mark on the nation.

Colored singing and playing artists are riding to fame and fortune with the current popular demand for "blues" disk recordings and because of the recognized fact that only a Negro can do justice to the native indigo ditties such artists are in great demand.
–Variety, July 26, 1923

Connie's, on Seventh Avenue at 182nd Street, is the first white outpost on the uptown colored frontier, the first stop on the route of the downtown night clubbers. Walk down one flight of stairs and you are in this rendezvous, so low ceilinged as to be cavelike. Around the dance floor is a three-foot barrier built in the semblance of a village, miniature bungalows and villas, and here and there a spired church, through the tiny windows of which comes the gleam of midget lights. If these lights in the windows remind any of the customers of home, sweet home they certainly show no outward signs of such tender thoughts in Connie's. You can tell Connie's is a high class joint as soon as you sit down, because the waiter usually whispers that bottles should be carried in the pocket, and not be placed on the floor.
–New York Daily News, November 1, 1929

To render a "Blues" song effectively, it is necessary to play the role of the oppressed or depressed, injecting into his or her rendition a spirit of hopeful prayer. "Blues" are more naturally blue when the melodic movements are treated with minor chords. It is possible to properly produce "Blues" effects on any instrument, although the wailings, moanings, and croonings, it can be understood, are more easily produced on instruments like the saxophone, trombone, or violin. Without the necessary moan, croon or slur, no blues number is properly sung.
–How to Play and Sing the Blues like the Phonograph and Stage Artists, a booklet by pianist Porter Grainger and arranger Bob Ricketts, 1926

Harlem has attained preeminence in the past few years as an amusement center. From midnight until after dawn it is a seething cauldron of Nubian mirth and hilarity. One sees as many limousines from Park and upper Fifth Avenue parked outside its sizzling cafes, "speaks," nightclubs and spiritual seances as in any other high-grade white locale in the country.
–Variety, October 16, 1929

What's jazz, lady? If you don't know, I can't tell you.
–Fats Waller to a white visitor to Harlem

Maude Russell leads her Ten Ebony Steppers through a lively number in
Just a Minute, one of many black shows that played Broadway.

DOMINO
REG. U.S. PAT. OFF.
15835
Fox Trot
ALABAMY BOUND
(Camino de Albany)
(De Sylva-Henderson)
CLUB WIGWAM ORCHESTRA
3458-A
DOMINO RECORD CO.
NEW YORK
MADE IN U.S.A.

Gennett
5292-A   8573
GRAVEYARD DREAM BLUES
(Cox)
Josie Miles with Piano Acc
DIVISION OF
THE STARR PIANO CO.
RICHMOND
IND.

Q·R·S
PRODUCTS
areBetter
Q·R·S
TRADE MARK
VOCAL—ORCH. A
DEATH STING ME BLUES
SARA MARTIN
Acc. by
CLARENCE WILLIAMS & HIS ORCHESTRA
R. 7042 — A
(278 — A)
Q·R·S Co. MANUFACTURE MUSIC ROLLS

Paramount
ELECTRICALLY   RECORDED
12486-A   For Dancing
Swamp Blues
Fletcher Henderson's
Orchestra
2827
IES INC ★ PORT WASHINGTON WIS ★ TRADE-MARK REGISTERED

OKeh
Reg. U.S. Pat. Off. March and September 2008 & 22 de Mayo al 1923
RECORDED BY TRUETONE PROCESS
8420-B
FOR BEST RESULT
USE OKeh NEF
PLEADIN' FOR THE BLUES
(Hill-Jones)
BERTHA "CHIPPIE" HILL
CONTRALTO, WITH PIANO
BY RICHARD M. JONES AND TRU
BY LOUIS ARMSTRONG
Recorded in Chicago
OKEH PHONOGRAPH CORPORATION

BLACK SWAN
RECORD
Formerly Number 14127-A
REG. U.S. PAT. OFF.
Paramount
12164-A
Blues Recor
Give Me That Old Slow Drag
(Tom Delaney)
Trixie Smith
and
The Jazz Masters
THIS RECORD IS MADE ENTIRELY IN OUR OWN LABORATORIES
THE NEW YORK RECORDING LABORATORIES
AT NEW YORK CITY AND GRAFTON, WISCONSIN. DUPLICATING
PORT W

Harmony
REG. U.S. PAT. OFF.
Fox Trot
MAKE ME KNOW IT
(Williams and Squires)
FESS WILLIAMS & HIS ROYAL
FLUSH SAVOY ORCHESTRA
(singing by Fess Williams)
189-H
(142244)
MADE AND PAT'D IN U.S.A. JAN. 21, '13 AND MAY 22, '23.

*Colorful labels marked
products of companies that
rushed to record the new
music—as performed by both
black artists and white imitators.*

An elegant George Gershwin puffs a cigar and makes musical notations in a 1927 portrait by famed photographer Edward Steichen.

Jazz Expands Its Boundaries

Perhaps the most celebrated musical event of the decade was the premier of George Gershwin's *Rhapsody in Blue* at Manhattan's Aeolian Hall in the winter of 1924. Many of New York's bluest blue bloods and all of its music critics practically stormed the old concert hall. Paul Whiteman, the chubby bandleader who conducted the *Rhapsody*, went out front before the concert started and saw a mob scene. "Men and women were fighting to get into the door," Whiteman reported, "pulling and mauling each other as they sometimes do at a baseball game, or a prize fight, or in the subway." The furor outlasted the concert; the critics either praised the music or damned it unmercifully. Deems Taylor, considered the dean of the critics, was for it. He found that the *Rhapsody* revealed "a genuine melodic gift and a piquant and individual harmonic sense." Taylor added, "Moreover, it is genuine jazz music."

It wasn't at all, of course—"symphonic jazz" perhaps, but not the real article. Nevertheless, though Gershwin didn't write jazz, he was the beau ideal of the Jazz Age. He was handsome, forceful, independent and charming—and he became quite rich. Above all he was spectacularly successful in an era that worshipped success. It was not quite rags to riches, although people often said it was. His parents were Russian immigrants, but Morris Gershowitz—that was the real family name—always had enough money for food, and even piano lessons. Nevertheless George had moved from a boyhood on the Lower East Side to the best salons of New York and London, where he hobnobbed with millionaires, duchesses and other celebrities of the time. And he was an undoubted genius at writing the show tunes that everybody whistled and hummed. Not just show tunes but whole shows full of them. And marvelous ones. They were original, fresh, clever, timely, and often quite beautiful—"Lady Be Good," "I've Got a Crush on You," "The Man I Love," "Someone to Watch Over Me," "Looking for a Boy" . . . the list could go on and on.

These tunes were not jazz (jazz was a way of performing music, rather than a way of writing it); but, ironically, many quickly became "jazz standards"—that is, tunes jazzmen loved to play and improvise around. Another irony of Gershwin's relationship with jazz is that he himself adored the music. As a boy of eight he would roller-skate through Harlem to 134th Street and sit on the curb outside Barron D. Wilkins's club and listen to that proto-jazz called ragtime float out the door. The first song on which he collaborated with his lyric-writing brother Ira proclaimed that "the great American folk song is a rag." His own piano playing had a very jazzy touch—angular, swift, offbeat. But he couldn't write the stuff, as the bemused critics and public thought. He was just a great songwriter, possibly the best that ever lived.

If Americans adored George Gershwin, they went absolutely (and inexplicably) mad for Paul Whiteman and his orchestra. A young violinist from Denver, Colorado, Whiteman came East in 1920 and by 1922 he could command $25,000 for a six-night engagement, an enormous sum at the time and one that was unmatched for decades. When he married a dancer named Vanda Hoff it was front-page news. When he went on a diet and managed to lose 100 pounds—normally his face and figure resembled comedian Oliver Hardy's—two books were written about his ordeal. The reason for this adulation is hard to imagine. Whiteman frequently had a topflight musician or two in his band (Bix Beiderbecke was one who played for him), but otherwise it was a mediocre outfit that burbled along without much beat, tone or imagination. Its popularity was, in short, a fad, an aberration of the dizzy decade. But there was nothing ephemeral about the real jazz, the glorious crazy-quilt of sound that spilled out of Barron Wilkins's and a thousand other joints to add the spice of originality to American music.

Paul Whiteman, baton in hand, conducts the so-called jazz
orchestra, strings and all, that galvanized the dancers of the '20s.

Panic roils Wall Street on October 24, 1929.

Boom and Bust
★
A NATION OF GAMBLERS

> "We have had booms and collapses in the past. But now we have no boom. Our progress is rapid—but sure. Buying is now larger than it ever was—but it is not frenzied. The kind of emotion which brings on a boom is absent."
>
> Samuel Crowther in *Collier's,* 1926

A 1921 cartoon entitled The Anglers shows shady operators fishing for victims in the stock exchange—a graphic warning widely ignored.

Business Fever

When President Coolidge declared in 1925 that "The business of America is business," he was putting it mildly—and belatedly. Three full years had passed since the end of the postwar recession, and business had become a national obsession. Everyone was spending avidly and the economy was spiraling upward at a record clip.

Production was up. The torrential output of consumer goods included such desirable new products as radios and electric refrigerators, along with countless improved models of standard items—faster cars, shinier bathroom fixtures, even plusher caskets.

Corporate profits were up. Thanks to new techniques of mass production, many manufacturers netted huge sums that they liberally plowed back into plant expansion. In 1923 U.S. Steel was operating so efficiently that it was able to reduce its workday from twelve to eight hours, to employ 17,000 additional workers, to raise wages and yet, amazingly, to show an increase in profits.

Income was up in most lines of endeavor. Even the industrial workers, whose strikes for higher pay had availed them little in the previous decade, benefited from company largesse and enjoyed a higher standard of living. To round out the happy picture, prices were stable; savings and life insurance doubled; and business was given added impetus by the growth of chain stores and installment buying. With all these factors reinforcing the upward spiral, prosperity seemed to have no ceiling.

In the full flush of fiscal euphoria, the country brought its swollen profits and abundant credit to bear in wild get-rich-quick speculation. By 1928 the prices of stocks had soared beyond the point of safe return as thousands of "little" people braved the hectic market seeking a share in overnight windfalls. A nurse made $30,000; a broker's valet amassed the tidy sum of a quarter-million.

At no time in the '20s were more than 1.5 million Americans involved in the market, but their much publicized successes fueled the reckless optimism of the country at large. Business, people came to believe, would provide everyone with a steadily increasing share of ever-expanding prosperity. It now seemed almost unpatriotic to exercise restraint in buying or to pay heed to the likes of economist Roger Babson, who warned: "Sooner or later a crash is coming, and it may be terrific." America was a nation of giddy consumers for whom wishful thinking had become a way of life.

The Radio Business

Of all the new products put on the market during the decade, none met with more spectacular success than the radio. As late as 1919, the radio audience was a scattering of avid hobbyists listening over earphones to barely audible crystal sets. Yet in the new decade radio quickly became a big business—twice over, in fact, as hardware for home entertainment and as a medium for advertising.

Radio had its practical beginning in 1920, when station KDKA in Pittsburgh announced the returns of the Harding-Cox Presidential election. Inspired by this modest triumph, KDKA began the first regularly scheduled broadcasting of news, church services and music. By the end of the decade, 618 stations were in business, and networks were regularly broadcasting from coast to coast.

The increasing availability of free home entertainment created a soaring demand for radios. Large-scale manufacturing operations began in 1920. Radio sales rose from less than two million dollars that year to $600 million in 1929.

At first, the airwaves were considered a public trust that must be kept unpolluted by commercialism. Even a trade journal for advertisers declared, "Any attempt to make the radio an advertising medium would, we think, prove positively offensive to great numbers of people." But that was in 1922, and in the same year the first sponsored program was broadcast over station WEAF in New York. The advertiser, a real estate corporation, was discreet enough, merely announcing itself as the sponsor without breathing a word in praise of its house lots. But this innocent precedent opened the floodgates.

The losing battle against commercial sponsorship was joined by Dr. Lee De Forest, whose invention of the three-element vacuum tube had helped make big-time radio possible. Long after radio programs had become firmly identified with sponsors' products, De Forest was still inveighing against advertising. "What have you done with my child? You have sent him out on the street in rags of ragtime to collect money from all and sundry. You have made of him a laughingstock of intelligence, surely a stench in the nostrils of the gods of the ionosphere."

Joining the radio craze, a shopper listens through earphones. The number of radio-owning families was 60,000 in 1922 and 13,750,000 in 1930.

Woolworth: 1920—1,111 stores; 1929—1,825 stores.

A & P: 1920—4,621 stores; 1929—15,418 stores.

J.C. Penney: 1920—312 stores; 1929—1,395 stores.

Standard Oil of New Jersey: 1920—12 stations; 1929—1,000 stations.

First National Stores: 1927—1,681 stores; 1929—2,002 stores.

Safeway Stores: 1926—766 stores; 1929—2,660 stores.

Western Auto Supply Co.: 1920—3 stores; 1929—54 stores.

Lerner Shops: 1920—6 stores; 1929—133 stores.

American Stores: 1920—1,243 stores; 1929—2,644 stores.

Piggly Wiggly: 1920—515 stores; 1929—2,500 stores.

S.S. Kresge: 1920—184 stores; 1929—597 stores.

United Cigar Stores: 1921—2,000 stores; 1929—3,700 stores.

Lengthening Chains

The average housewife of the '20s knew little about the merchandising revolution that was spreading networks of chain stores from coast to coast. But she had a keen appreciation of the advantages offered by fast-growing chains (*left*) in many fields. Canned pears from Bohack's, a lunch of pancakes at Childs, aspirin from a United Drug store, a summer frock from Lerner's, an oil change at an Esso station and Fanny Farmer mints—all such chain items had some special attraction, be it lower price, wider selection, greater reliability, better service or simply convenience and familiarity.

For the housewife and the chain alike, economy was the ruling passion. Chains cut costs through volume purchasing and heightened efficiency, and passed on a part of the saving to the consumer. The gigantic A & P chain, which bought a half-billion dozen eggs a year, could afford to set its price per dozen several cents lower than that of the small-scale independent grocery—the so-called "Ma and Pa" operation. Comparable cost-price benefits stemmed from a different source at the F.W. Woolworth Company. Its 1,500 five-and-ten-cent stores were stocked with rewarding economy by only 36 expert buyers.

Salary savings were even more important to a trailblazing company in the fiercely competitive grocery business, which was crowded with 860 rival chains by 1928. This particular firm, Piggly Wiggly, featured a method of operation new to the field at the start of the decade. Under the proud slogan "Scientific Merchandising," Piggly Wiggly created a self-service system, with its markets laid out according to a patented traffic pattern. The stores—the first supermarkets—were popularly known as grocerterias until the handier term was coined.

The self-service format worked spectacularly well. Piggly Wiggly boasted the nation's highest average sales per customer. Reflecting and insuring its success were prices that undercut larger chains with greater purchasing power. In 1921 Piggly Wiggly offered three pounds of a national-brand coffee for $1.05, while a conventional service store charged $1.55. Even A & P, the biggest egg merchant of them all, could not match the Piggly Wiggly price of 36 cents a dozen. If thrift was demanded by a housewife's budget, she scrambled eggs purveyed by Piggly Wiggly.

For all the battles fought between chains and independents, decisive victories were few and far between, but a resounding triumph was won in the movie-theater field, and it revamped the young industry. In earlier, harder times for the trade, film producers licensed their movies for exhibition through distributors to theater owners; the three parties were, for the most part, separate interests. But as movies became more popular, costly and profitable, a natural trend toward consolidation swiftly developed. By 1922 average weekly theater admissions totaled 40 million, and the figure doubled in the next seven years. This business—at ticket prices never less than 10 cents and often more than 75 cents at first-run theaters—was very big business, well worth fighting for.

The movie makers, being the source of the lucrative product, started with the upper hand, and were able to rig their policies so as to overwhelm and take over many distributors. The big producers also bought up theaters, as much to shut out their rivals' films as to make more money

Loew's Paradise, a victim of Bronx zoning, lacked the usual marquee.

exhibiting their own. In the dog-eat-dog struggle to assemble big chains, one of the sharpest sets of teeth belonged to the brilliant head of Paramount, Adolph Zukor, whose goal was nothing short of a complete monopoly. Using stealthy mergers and brute cash freely, Zukor snapped up theaters singly and in whole chains, and acquired small producers to boot. More and more theaters fell into fewer and fewer hands. By 1927 the field was practically denuded of important independents. The nation's 20,000 theaters, along with some 600 distributors, had been forged into a few long chains owned or controlled by great producers.

During and after the war for existing outlets, new theaters were built at a frantic rate, and these, like the theater chains, got bigger and richer steadily. The movie palaces of the '20s were just that, palaces—edifices as huge and lavish as the celluloid dreams they offered. The really big theaters, such as the Roxy in New York and the Fox in Detroit, seated some 5,000 people. New York's Capitol Theater, seating 5,300, was so cavernous that a movie magazine remarked, "The mezzanine floor looks as if it had been designed for eight-day bicycle races."

Everything in these deluxe palaces was on an inflated scale. Vast and opulent accommodations overawed the customer: imperial staircases, kingly rest rooms, princely chambers for depositing children in an attendant's care. Gilded ornaments, sumptuous rugs, marble statuary, ponderous crystal chandeliers, epic murals, and ceilings painted with fleecy clouds—these and other sensations were laid on with a trowel. Every imaginable style of architecture and decoration was used in one theater or another, and sometimes many of them could be discerned in a single theater. Indeed the taste for flamboyance was dignified by stylistic titles hitherto unknown: the San Francisco Fox *(right),* one of several palaces decorated by Fox's wife Eve Leo, was said to be an outstanding example of "Early Eve Leo."

The spectacular lobby of the San Francisco Fox had its own pipe organ, atop the grand staircase, to regale moviegoers awaiting the next show.

In Loew's Paradise, 3,936 customers could enjoy the movie in comfort amid a veritable museum of Renaissance-like statuary in gilded niches.

The Golden Dawn of Total Advertising

Lionized and romanticized, the advertising men of the '20s were prone to forget how far their vocation had come since the turn of the century. In that dim recent past, advertising's function remained primarily and politely informative—to describe a product interestingly, lest potential customers fail to buy out of abysmal ignorance. But in the new go-getter spirit of the age, the soft sell hardened as competition increased apace with the volume and variety of manufactured goods. Concurrently, the mass-marketing revolution broke down the lingering vestiges of regional merchandising, making it possible to advertise national brands in national magazines—this with the newly added impact of full-color printing. Thus the great postwar boom ushered in the age of all-out advertising. By 1925 the magazines and newspapers owed 70 percent of their total income of $1.3 billion to ad revenue.

Under the tempering heat of competition, the modern advertising agency emerged in the '20s as a sophisticated team of high-paid specialists. Ad agencies earned their commissions by doing far more than creating and placing ads; their various experts often named, packaged, priced and promoted the distribution of the product. Great ad men could, and did, bestow instant success on fledgling products and sick businesses. Albert Lasker, the brilliant owner of the Lord & Thomas agency, was largely responsible in 1920 for selling America a rather shopworn firm and its untested new product—the Republican party and Warren G. Harding.

Marking the ads of the '20s were several traits that they shared with the decade itself, such as brashness and a lack of scruples. Many ads trafficked in quasi-factual, pseudoscientific details: a mouthwash boasted the approval of exactly 45,512 doctors, none of them named; and a shaving cream stated with weighty significance that it expanded 250 times upon contact with water. Another phenomenon was the popularity of testimonial ads, which brought fees of up to $5,000 to celebrities in every field.

But the decade's dominant and identifying trend in advertising was the increasing use of psychology, the deepening appeal to the secret emotions that motivated people to buy. If any single ad epitomized the trend and solemnized its acceptance, it was Ned Jordan's 173-word classic, "Somewhere West of Laramie" (opposite).

Jordan was a copywriter-turned-manufacturer: trained in the "nuts-and-bolts" school of auto advertising, he had given in to an urge to produce cars himself. One day he caught a glimpse of a custom-built roadster that showman Flo Ziegfeld had ordered for actress Billie Burke, and on the strength of rough sketches he raised $400,000, capital enough to buy parts and assemble some rakish, aluminum-bodied cars. Then Jordan launched his ad.

"Somewhere West of Laramie" broke all the rules. It offered no data on the Jordan's brakes or carburetor; it made no grandiose claims of power or elegance. But the ad firmly planted in the readers' minds a connection between the Jordan and a pleasant feeling of freedom, excitement, romantic adventure. That was enough. Jordan's cars were too costly to sell in volume, but, as Jordan later said, "We *did* make a lot of money *awfully* fast."

As the decade wore on, psychological insights—particularly the realization that fear was a wonderful persuader—were applied with increasing effectiveness, as shown by the ads on following pages. The practice was not, to be sure, admired by everyone. But even the malcontents agreed with a cheerful squib in the Kansas City *Journal-Post:* "Advertising and mass production are the twin cylinders that keep the motor of modern business in motion."

Jordan's famous ad (opposite, upper left) used poetic prose to glamorize its cars, while slogans old and new became familiar through repetition, making household names of brands such as Coca-Cola, Chesterfield and Palmolive.

Somewhere West of Laramie

SOMEWHERE west of Laramie there's a broncho-busting, steer-roping girl who knows what I'm talking about.

She can tell what a sassy pony, that's a cross between greased lightning and the place where it hits, can do with eleven hundred pounds of steel and action when he's going high, wide and handsome.

The truth is—the Playboy was built for her.

Built for the lass whose face is brown with the sun when the day is done of revel and romp and race.

She loves the cross of the wild and the tame.

There's a savor of links about that car—of laughter and lilt and light—a hint of old loves—and saddle and quirt. It's a brawny thing—yet a graceful thing for the sweep o' the Avenue.

Step into the Playboy when the hour grows dull with things gone dead and stale.

Then start for the land of real living with the spirit of the lass who rides, lean and rangy, into the red horizon of a Wyoming twilight.

JORDAN

JORDAN MOTOR CAR COMPANY, Inc., Cleveland, Ohio

I'll tell the world

They Satisfy

Chesterfield
CIGARETTES

—and the blend can't be copied

The pause that refreshes

Drink **Coca-Cola**
Delicious and Refreshing

The Coca-Cola Company, Atlanta, Ga.

EACH busy day tends down hill from that top-of-the-morning feeling with which you begin. Don't whip yourself as the day begins to wear. Pause and refresh yourself with an ice-cold Coca-Cola, and be off to a fresh start. ▼ ▼ ▼ The wholesome refreshment of Coca-Cola has made it the one great drink of the millions. A perfect blend of many flavors, it has

a flavor all its own—delicious to taste and, more than that, with a cool after-sense of refreshment. ▼ ▼ ▼ It is ready, cold and tingling, at fountains and refreshment stands around the corner from anywhere.

THE BEST SERVED DRINK IN THE WORLD

A pure drink of natural flavors served ice-cold in its own bottle—the distinctive Coca-Cola bottle. Every bottle is sterilized, filled and sealed air-tight by automatic machines, without the touch of human hands—insuring purity and wholesomeness.

OVER **8** MILLION A DAY

IT HAD TO BE GOOD   TO GET WHERE IT IS

Naturally Lovable

"That Schoolgirl Complexion"

—is kept and safeguarded by thousands through following this simple rule in daily skin care

MODERN beauty culture, today, starts largely with choosing a bland complexion soap.

That's the reason millions use Palmolive —a soap made solely to safeguard the skin. In America, it is the largest selling toilet soap. In France, it is one of the two largest — the "imported" soap in beauty-wise Paris, that is supplanting French soaps by the score!

Palmolive is a beauty soap. A soap made of bland and soothing cosmetic oils, solely for one purpose; to safeguard the complexion. A soap made to be used freely, lavishly on the skin.

Used in the following way, it is confined with more beautiful skins, probably, than any other beauty method. Its results you see on every side today.

The rule to follow if guarding a good complexion is your goal

Wash your face gently with soothing Palmolive

AS more women become skilled in the ways of beauty, more and more turn to natural ways in skin care.

That means a clean skin; pores kept free of accumulations to perform their functions *naturally*.

Thus modern beauty culture starts with soap and water; its only secret being the KIND of SOAP one uses—and how.

soap, massaging the lather softly into the skin. Rinse thoroughly, first with warm water, then with cold. If your skin is inclined to be dry, apply a touch of good cold cream—that is all. Do this regularly, and particularly in the evening. Use powder and rouge if you wish. But never leave them on over night. They clog the pores, often enlarge them, Blackheads and disfigurements often follow. They must be washed away.

Avoid this mistake

Do not use ordinary soaps in the treatment given above. Do not think any green soap, or one represented as of olive and palm oils, is the same as Palmolive.

And it costs but 10c the cake! So little that millions let it do for their bodies what it does for their faces. Obtain a cake today. Then note the amazing difference one week makes. The Palmolive Company (Del. Corp.), Chicago, Ill.

PALMOLIVE

Retail Price 10c

Palmolive Soap is untouched by human hands until you break the wrapper—it is never sold unwrapped.

KEEP THAT SCHOOLGIRL COMPLEXION

Oh, memories that bless and burn . . .

Sometimes, when lights are low, they come back to comfort and at the same time sadden her—those memories of long ago, when she was a slip of a girl in love with a dark-eyed Nashville boy. They were the happiest moments of her life—those days of courtship. Though she had never married, no one could take from her the knowledge that she had been loved passionately, devotedly; those frayed and yellowed letters of his still told her so. How happy and ambitious they had been for their future together. And then, like a stab, came their parting . . . the broken engagement . . . the sorrow and the shock of it. She could find no explanation for it then, and now, in the soft twilight of life when she can think calmly, it is still a mystery to her.

Are you sure about yourself?

How often some trivial gesture, habit or fault alters the course of human affairs. On every side you hear of engagements broken for trifling causes. Of marriages that ride into the divorce court on the strange complaint "incompatibility."

If you have ever come face to face with a real case of halitosis (unpleasant breath) you can understand how it might well be an obstacle to pleasant business, professional, and social relations.

The insidious thing about halitosis is that you never know when you have it. It does not announce itself to the victim. Important to remember also, is the fact that few people escape it entirely. That is because every day in any

normal mouth, conditions capable of causing halitosis are likely to arise.

Common causes are: Stomach derangements due to excesses of eating or drinking, fermenting food particles in the mouth, defective or decaying teeth, pyorrhea, catarrh, and infections of the nose, mouth or throat.

The pleasant way to put your breath beyond

suspicion, is to rinse the mouth with full strength Listerine, the safe antiseptic. Every morning. Every night. And between times before meeting others.

Being antiseptic, Listerine checks food fermentation. Being also a remarkable germicide,* it attacks infection from which odors spring. Finally, being a deodorant, it destroys the odors themselves, leaving both mouth and breath fresh, sweet, and clean. Lambert Pharmacal Company, St. Louis, Mo., U. S. A.

LISTERINE
ends halitosis

*Though safe to use in any body cavity, full strength Listerine kills even the resistant Staphylococcus Aureus (pus) and Bacillus Typhosus (typhoid) germs in counts ranging to 200,000,000 in 15 seconds. (Fastest time science has accurately recorded.)

The Self-improvement Pitch

Many an ad of the '20s suggested to the reader that he had woeful weaknesses or repellent traits that only the advertised product could remedy. Listerine mouthwash, for example, pledged to save one from an old maid's loneliness (left) caused by unpleasant breath. According to the publishers of Dr. Eliot's Five-Foot Shelf, a reader need spend only 15 minutes a day browsing pleasurably through the classics in order to achieve great popularity as a wise, sparkling conversationalist. This promise was the last straw to one writer wearied by the mail-order panaceas. He replied in a satire for the humor magazine Life: "I am still worried because the other 23 hours and 45 minutes are going to drag so dreadfully."

> "And then, like a stab, came their parting... the broken engagement ...the sorrow and the shock of it. She could find no explanation for it then, and now, in the soft twilight of life when she can think calmly, it is still a mystery to her."

Listerine ad attributing a spinster's loneliness to halitosis

Snob Appeal

The consumer was often urged to buy a certain product because it was fashionable—i.e., preferred by people of wealth, position and savoir-faire. Many an ad depicted elegant folk in formal attire on some unlikely pilgrimage: down to the cellar to enjoy the clean heat provided by the American Radiator Company, into the kitchen to admire a General Electric refrigerator. In the case of bathrooms, the Crane Company suggested that its fixtures defined true "chic." Of course, bathrooms were only as fashionable as they were costly; the average wage earner might shell out three months' pay for the finest "shrine of cleanliness and health." In case he already had one such shrine, some ads strongly indicated that he needed another.

Cheesecake in the Ads

As changing fashions exposed more and more of the female form, the trend was recorded—and accelerated—by daring advertisers. Among the leaders was the Holeproof Hosiery Company, whose ads helped transform silk stockings from a sheer luxury to an impractical necessity. The display of silk-clad limbs proved to be such an eye-catcher that it was used to advertise many other products. This practice called forth a facetious protest from a female wit, who said of mail-order ads, "If you accept the invitation to 'Sign Here Today,' under a pair of silk stockings, what a miscellany of articles will come parcel-posting unexpectedly into your front hall. Beaver board for walls and ceilings! Electric washing machines! A new kind of raisin pie!"

Holeproof Hosiery

COLES PHILLIPS

HOLEPROOF is the hosiery of lustrous beauty and fine texture that wears so well. It is not surprising, therefore, that it is selected by many people who can afford to pay far more for their hose, but who prefer the Holeproof combination of style and serviceability at such reasonable prices.

Obtainable in Pure Silk, Silk Faced, and Lusterized Lisle styles for men, women and children in the season's popular colors. If your dealer cannot supply you, write for price list and illustrated booklet.

HOLEPROOF HOSIERY COMPANY, Milwaukee, Wisconsin
Holeproof Hosiery Company of Canada, Limited, London, Ontario   © H. H. Co.

The Boom Goes Bust

In November 1929, soon after the stock market crash, a New York policeman found a bedraggled parrot. In a fitting epitaph to the disaster, the bird kept squawking, "More margin! More margin!"

The lack of more margin was the straw that broke the back of the Big Bull Market and signaled the end of the Coolidge-Hoover prosperity. Before the market cracked, stocks were not only priced far above their real value; they were being bought for a marginal down payment of as little as 10 percent, with the bulk of the purchase price financed by brokers' loans. As stock prices slumped, overextended investors were required to put up additional margin, and many could produce the capital only by selling off shares at distress prices. This drove the market into a steeper, broader descent—and redoubled the brokers' demands for margin. Between late October and mid-November, stocks lost more than 40 percent of their total valuation—a drop of $30 billion in paper values.

Those few weeks were a nightmare. Market-wise reporters struggled in vain to describe adequately the pandemonium on the stock exchange floor. Only slowly, as personal anecdotes fleshed out the appalling statistics, did the scope of the Crash become amply evident. One woman, presented by her broker with an enormous bill for more margin, cried out in bewilderment, "How could I lose $100,000? I never had $100,000." Facing the mad scramble to obtain margin money, pawnbrokers had to turn away hundreds seeking loans on jewelry.

October 29, when stocks suffered their worst losses, was catastrophic for almost everyone but a shrewd (and possibly apocryphal) messenger boy. Noting that a big block of White Sewing Machine stock was being offered at any price with no takers, he allegedly snapped it up at a dollar a share.

In an effort to bolster confidence, John D. Rockefeller announced, "My son and I have for some days been pur-chasing sound common stocks." A spirited rejoinder came from one of many hard-hit celebrities, comedian Eddie Cantor: "Sure, who else had any money left?"

The president of Union Cigar, stunned when his company's stock plummeted from $113.50 to four dollars in a day, fell or jumped to his death from the ledge of a New York hotel. Tales of suicide became standard fare in the mythology of the Crash. Actually, the suicide rate was higher in the few months before the Crash than in those just after it. Still, thousands of people had lost everything but their lives, and there was much truth to one man's remark that, while Jerusalem had only one Wailing Wall, "in Wall Street every wall is wet with tears."

In the aftermath, the country seemed to pause with bated breath while its leaders formed opinions. Their confident verdicts were not long in coming. Said President Hoover: "The fundamental business of the country, that is, production and distribution of commodities, is on a sound and prosperous basis."

But certain conditions, visible for months to anyone who put aside his rose-colored glasses, told quite another story: the economy was basically unsound. Banks and corporations were structurally weak and in many cases undermined by skullduggery and fraud. America's trade policies were self-defeating. The market for consumer goods was both glutted and untapped: 90 percent of the nation's wealth was concentrated in the hands of only 13 percent of the people; meanwhile, large depressed segments of society—among them farmers, textile workers and coal miners—lacked sufficient income to buy much more than their minimal needs. In its relation to these and other unhealthy symptoms, the stock market crash was far more than a private retribution for greedy speculators. It was a clear warning for all.

Yet most of the pundits held that prospects were bright, and everyone wanted to believe the good word. Tentatively reassured, people resumed their business pursuits, tried to recapture their boom-time zest for getting and spending. But somehow things were not quite the same.

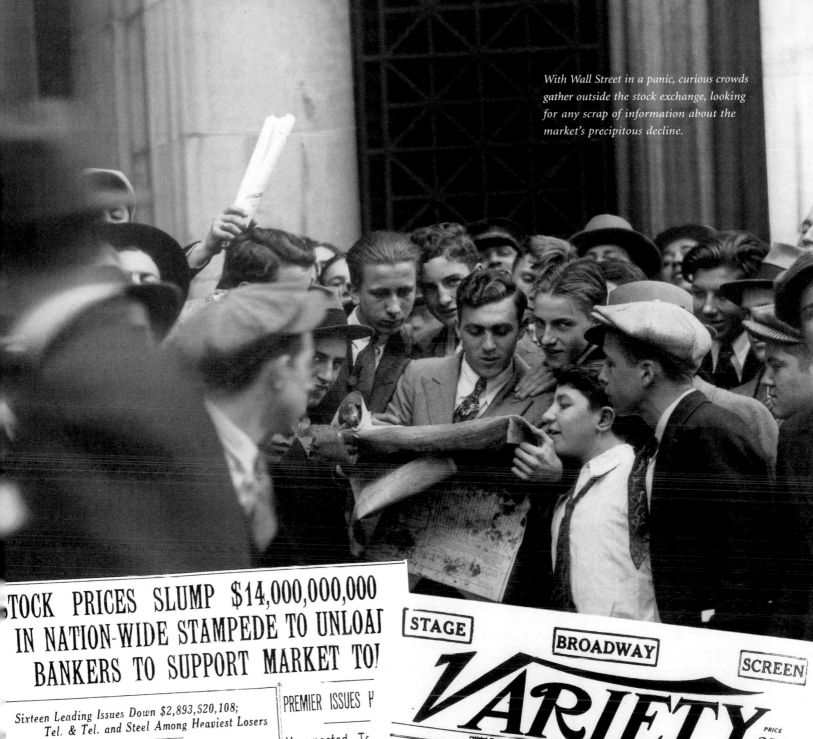

With Wall Street in a panic, curious crowds gather outside the stock exchange, looking for any scrap of information about the market's precipitous decline.

STOCK PRICES SLUMP $14,000,000,000
IN NATION-WIDE STAMPEDE TO UNLOAD
BANKERS TO SUPPORT MARKET TO[

Sixteen Leading Issues Down $2,893,520,108; Tel. & Tel. and Steel Among Heaviest Losers

A shrinkage of $2,893,520,108 in the open market value of the shares of sixteen representative companies resulted from yesterday's sweeping decline on the New York Stock Exchange.

American Telephone and Telegraph was the heaviest loser, $448,905,162 having been lopped off of its total value. United States Steel common, traditional bellwether of the stock market, made its greatest nose-dive in recent years by falling from a high of 202½ to a low of 185. In a feeble last-minute rally it snapped back to 186,

PREMIER ISSUES H

Unexpected To
Liquidation
Rocks Ma

STAGE   BROADWAY   SCREEN

VARIETY   PRICE 25¢

VOL. XCVII. No. 3   NEW YORK, WEDNESDAY, OCTOBER 30, 1929   88 PAGES

WALL ST. LAYS AN EGG

RST STOCK CRASH STEMMED BY BANKS;
[,]894,650-SHARE DAY SWAMPS MARKET;
[L]EADERS CONFER, FIND CONDITIONS SOUND

STOCKS COLLAPSE IN 16,410,03[0
BUT RALLY AT CLOSE CHEE[
BANKERS OPTIMISTIC, TO C[

[ERS] EASE TENSION

[Wa]ll Street Bankers [i]d Two Meetings at Morgan Office.

Wall Street Optimistic After Stormy Day; Clerical Work May Force Holiday Tomorrow

Confidence in the soundness of the stock market structure, notwithstanding the upheaval of the last few days, was voiced last night by bankers and other financial leaders. Sentiment as expressed by the heads of some of the largest banking institutions and by industrial executives as well was distinctly cheerful and the feeling was general that the worst had been seen. Wall Street ended the day in an optimistic frame of mind.

LOSSES RECOVERED IN PART

Upward Trend Start[With 200,000-Share Order for Steel.

LEADERS SEE FEAR WANING

Point to 'Lifting Spells' in Trading as Sign of Buying Activity.

240 Issues Lose $15,894,818,894 in Month; Slump in Full Exchange List Vastly Large[r

The drastic effects of Wall Street's October bear market i[s] shown by valuation tables prepared last night by THE NEW YORK TIMES, which place the decline in the market value of 240 represen[t]ative issues on the New York Stock Exchange at $15,894,818,89[4] during the period from Oct. 1 to yesterday's clos[e]. [...] are 1,279 issues listed on the New York Stock Exchange.

All cameras are focused on Babe Ruth at the 1921 World Series.

An Era of Giants

This was the heroic era of American sports. Attendance at athletic events broke all records, and the champions of sport were known and loved throughout the land. "If St. Paul were living today," a prominent Methodist minister declared, "he would know Babe Ruth's batting average and what yardage Red Grange made."

And that applied to many others besides Ruth and Grange. Jack Dempsey, the grim Manassa Mauler, came out of the West to give boxing its first million-dollar gates. Bobby Jones and Bill Tilden took golf and tennis away from the country-club crowd and made them "important" sports. Swimmer Gertrude Ederle, Helen Wills, a tennis player, and golfer Glenna Collett showed that a woman's place was also in the sports pages.

One reason for the heightened interest in sport was the sudden emergence of the sports writer as a major figure on the literary scene—men such as Grantland Rice, Damon Runyon, Ring Lardner, Paul Gallico, John Kieran and Westbrook Pegler. These experts were occasionally assisted by outsiders like H. L. Mencken and even George Bernard Shaw (Shaw described the game of baseball as a combination of the "best features of that primitive form of cricket known as Tip and Run with those of lawn tennis, Puss-in-the-Corner, and Handel's *Messiah*.") The great writers recorded the deeds of the great athletes. One early beneficiary was that giant of giants, Babe Ruth. "After the Black Sox scandal," wrote W. O. McGeehan, "Babe Ruth with his bat pounded baseball back into popularity. He swings with the utmost sincerity. When he hits the ball it goes into wide-open spaces. When he misses, he misses with vehement sincerity."

By 1927, when he hit his high-water mark of 60 home runs, Babe Ruth was a better-known American to most foreigners than Calvin Coolidge, and he rivaled the dashing Prince of Wales as the most photographed man in the world. Kieran was moved to this bit of hero-worshipping doggerel, typical of the sports-page exaggeration of the era: "My voice may be loud above the crowd / And my words just a bit uncouth, / But I'll stand and shout till the last man's out: / 'There never was a guy like Ruth!'"

The fact that the Babe was himself a bit uncouth—a wencher, imbiber, and notorious violator of training rules—bothered neither the writers nor the fans. He was simply the greatest ballplayer who ever lived, and he symbolized as no other man ever did the love affair that existed between the American public and the athletes of the 1920s.

"I see them walk by in a dream—Dempsey and Cobb and Ruth, Tunney and Sande and Jones—Johnson and Matty and Young—Alex and Tilden and Thorpe—was there a flash of youth that gave us a list like this, when our first tributes were sung?"

Grantland Rice

Paul Gallico wrote of Ruth: "There has always been a magic about that gross, ugly, coarse, Gargantuan figure of a man and everything he did."

The Supreme Swimmers

In 1926, when 19-year-old Gertrude Ederle swam the English Channel, it was front-page news across the nation. Not only was "Our Trudy" the first woman to conquer the Channel, but her time—14 hours and 31 minutes—was almost two hours faster than the men's record. She was lionized with a huge ticker-tape parade when she returned to New York. The excerpt below, from the *New York Herald Tribune*, shows the esteem in which Trudy was held at her peak. But by the following year she was slipping into obscurity and the headlines once more belonged to handsome swimming idol Johnny Weissmuller *(opposite)*. Between 1921 and 1929—when he "retired" from competition at the age of 24—Weissmuller set some 67 records.

If there is one woman who can make the swim, it is this girl, with the shoulders and back of Jack Dempsey and the frankest and bravest pair of eyes that ever looked into a face. She told me of her last attempt, when she swam for an hour on instinct alone, blinded, deaf and only half conscious. She remembered only the humor of the trip. This girl keeps her even temper. I felt that I would sooner be in that tug the day she starts than at the ringside of the greatest fight or at the arena of the greatest game in the world, for this, in my opinion, is to be the greatest sports story in the world.

—W.O. McGeehan

Gertrude Ederle dons grease to ward off the cold before swimming the English Channel in 1926.

Johnny Weissmuller, never beaten in any freestyle race from 100 yards to a half mile, set a world record for 100 meters at the 1924 Olympic Games.

Red Grange, shown as a pro player, said, "The same fellows who advised me not to play professional wouldn't lend me a dollar if I were broke."

The Rock and the Redhead

Until the '20s, a fair number of Eastern sports writers believed that the only brand of college football worth writing about was played on the gridirons of Harvard, Yale and Princeton. And then along came Knute Rockne *(right)* and Red Grange out of the Midwest to change their minds.

Rockne's superbly coached Notre Dame teams won 105 games and lost only 12 between 1919 and 1931. His locker-room exhortations became football lore; but his real renown rested on his ability to find—and make—fine football players. Four of the best were on his 1924 team; after that year's win over Army, in an effort to describe the small, swift Notre Dame backfield, Grantland Rice typed: "Outlined against a blue-gray October sky, the Four Horsemen rode again. In dramatic lore they are known as Famine, Pestilence, Destruction and Death. These are only aliases. Their real names are Stuhldreher, Miller, Crowley and Layden."

But even the best players Rockne could produce were overshadowed by Red Grange, the "Galloping Ghost" of Illinois. A three-time All-American, Grange helped dedicate Illinois' new stadium in 1924 by personally demolishing a fine Michigan team with touchdown runs of 95, 67, 55 and 45 yards the first four times he carried the ball. Within hours after he stripped off his famous No. 77 jersey for the last time in 1925, Grange signed a contract to play professionally. "I do not like football well enough to play it for nothing," he explained. Playing it for about $1,000 a minute, Grange was a millionaire in just three years.

After his team had taken a first-half shellacking and sat waiting for the blast, Rockne merely poked his head in the door of the dressing room and remarked quietly, "Oh, excuse me, ladies! I thought this was the Notre Dame team."
–Paul Gallico

What a football player—this man Red Grange. He is melody and symphony. He is crashing sound. He is brute force.
–Damon Runyon

Dempsey's Last Shot

T he greatest prize fight of the decade occurred at Chicago's Soldier Field on September 22, 1927. The principals were the aging challenger, Jack Dempsey, and heavyweight champion Gene Tunney, a methodical boxer four years younger who liked to quote Shakespeare.

Dempsey and Tunney had met once before, a year earlier, when Dempsey had been the cocky champion, Tunney the challenger. But when that fight was over, Dempsey was a battered loser. His refusal to alibi his defeat was cherished by ring fans. ("What happened?" asked his dismayed wife, actress Estelle Taylor. "Honey," said Dempsey, "I forgot to duck.")

The 1927 rematch, billed as "The Battle of the Ages," actually was a dull fight until the seventh round. Then Dempsey, with his old vigor, made a bid for victory—described on the opposite page in a *New York Times* story—only to commit a blunder that resulted in a controversy: did Tunney get the benefit of a "long count" or did he win fair and square?

At 32, Dempsey (right, above) still packed a wallop in his right, called "Iron Mike."

Tunney (right), whose goal was to lick Dempsey, quit undefeated in 1928.

Dempsey, plunging in recklessly, suddenly lashed a long, wicked left to the jaw. This he followed with a right to the jaw, the old "Iron Mike" as deadly as ever, and quickly drove another left hook to the jaw, under which Tunney toppled like a falling tree. The challenging ex-champion stood there in his own corner, the characteristic Dempsey snarl o'erspreading his countenance, his expression saying more plainly than words: "Get up and I'll knock you down again." Finally Dempsey took cognizance of the referee's frantic motions and sped across the ring to a neutral corner. But three or four, or possibly five precious seconds elapsed. Tunney got to his feet with the assistance of ring ropes and with visible effort at the count of "nine." He was groggy. But Dempsey was wild, a floundering plodding mankiller as Tunney, backpedaling for dear life, took to full flight. The former champion stopped dead in his tracks in mid-ring and with a smile spreading over his scowling face, motioned disgustedly for Tunney to come on and fight. But Tunney was playing his own game and it was a winning game.
–James P. Dawson

A crowd of 104,942 paid a record $2,658,600 to watch the fight, while about 50 million Americans listened to Graham McNamee's ringside radio description.

The Reign of Big Bill

William Tatem Tilden II, the greatest tennis player of the decade, once wrote: "The player owes the gallery as much as an actor owes an audience." It was typical of Big Bill to link tennis and the theater, the two worlds he loved most. Purists might complain that he did too much acting on the court—holding aloft an injured finger or playing with his sweater on for a set or two before peeling it off for the blazing finish—but the generation of fans that Tilden created loved every scene. Alas, Big Bill was a better actor on the tennis court than he was on the stage. He spent a small fortune bankrolling plays in which he was the star. But none of them had tennis scenes, which may explain why all of them were flops.

Big Bill was all of 27 years old, a ripe old age in competitive tennis, when he won his first national singles championship in 1920 and he was still going strong when he added championship No. 7 at the age of 36. A famous columnist, writing in *Collier's* in 1922, caught the full flavor of Tilden's artistic temperament in the following excerpt.

It seems as though Tilden often says to himself: "This is going to be a hard match." Coming to play, he finds it easy. So he makes it hard. He loses a set or two, usually electrifying the gallery in the winning of the match. "Playing to the stands," say his legion of sneering commentators. I am certain that he would play exactly the same game, saying the same "Oh, rotten" when he misses an easy one, if the court were in a back yard somewhere, with nobody to see it at all. His "Oh, Gerald!" and "Peach, Bill!" are sincere expressions of admiration, though sometimes the gallery thinks his meaning is "Any shot I can't get is a daisy." He doesn't mean that, but it is true. Anybody who aces Tilden has to do it with a perfect shot.
–Franklin P. Adams

A slim six-footer, Bill Tilden never weighed more than 165 pounds.

"Little Miss Poker Face"

Helen Wills was everything that Bill Tilden was not: cool, aloof, expressionless, efficient and consumed with the single idea of being the best woman amateur tennis player in the world. But although she won her first national title in 1923, at the age of 17, she did not achieve her goal world-wide until 1927—and then by a quirk. That was the year glamorous French star Suzanne Lenglen—who a short time before had defeated Miss Wills—kept the Queen of England waiting for half an hour at Wimbledon, creating an international incident that made it highly expedient for her to turn professional. Most writers bemoaned the departure of La Lenglen, a witty and uninhibited champion, more than they hailed the advent of "Queen Helen," who methodically won every match she entered from 1927 to the end of the decade.

But even though the writers dubbed her "Little Miss Poker Face," they had a reluctant admiration for the regal Californian, as the contemporary report below indicates.

Helen Wills goes about the business of tennis as calmly as an etcher making a design. Suzanne Lenglen cannot play unless people are watching; the little brown moons under her eyes suggest that she has come to the court without sleep after a night of carnival. Miss Wills, in their third set, was three games ahead of the Frenchwoman. Mlle. Lenglen was obviously tiring. She went to the sidelines and asked for a glass of brandy. Helen Wills lost the match. She would not, matching drink for drink, implore the gods of a strange land.

Masculinity characterizes the Wills game. Whenever she can she practices with a man, because "it is the best training, the men are naturally more strong, though not always so deft."
–Time

Helen Wills, never fast, used a powerful serve to wear out opponents.

"De Mostest Hoss"

The sports writers dubbed him "Big Red," but his groom, Will Harbut, called him "de mostest hoss" and that was a better description of Man O'War. He was an amazing combination of size (1,150 pounds) and speed (five American records in 1920 alone), with an appetite so great that he reportedly was fed with a bit in his mouth to slow down his eating. Man O'War won 20 of his 21 starts in 1919 and 1920; at least once he ran away from the field by 100 lengths, a figure in keeping with the odds in his favor, which three times reached 1 to 100. In the one race he lost—to a horse named, naturally, Upset—he was victimized by a poor start and was gaining rapidly at the finish. Earl Sande, the premier jockey of the decade, rode Man O'War only once and never forgot it. "That day, I knew I was riding the greatest horse ever bred for running," he said. The *New York Tribune* ran the following account of Man O'War's most exciting victory in 1920.

Man O'War proved himself the horse of eternity at Aqueduct yesterday afternoon. Lucky indeed was he who can say he saw Man O'War on July 10, 1920. He saw the greatest race of turf history won by the greatest horse. But for this super-horse, John P. Grier might today be heralded as the equine champion of the age. He ran a race that would have beaten any horse that ever looked through a bridle—except Man O'War. From start to finish, every post of the journey was passed in record time. And until almost the very end it seemed that Grier might win. For the first time in his racing career the sleek chestnut sides of Man O'War felt the cut of the whip. Bummer applied the lash with right good will. And Man O'War, roused to the idea that something vital was at stake, responded as the great horse that he is. He charged at his rival with all the power of his marvellous frame and simply broke the heart of as game a three-year-old as this country will see in many a day.
–W. J. Macbeth

Man O'War's giant stride ate up 27 feet at every leap, and the jockey's job often was to pace the big horse when he tried to run all out.

The King and Queen of Golf

Bobby Jones's feat of winning the world's four major golf tournaments in 1930—the unprecedented "Grand Slam"—concluded an amazing run of success a biographer called Jones's "eight fat years." In that time he won 13 national championships on both sides of the Atlantic. But before then, Jones *(left)* struggled through "seven lean years," when he failed to win a single big tournament. At the 1921 British Open, he blew up in memorable fashion and shocked the spectators by picking up his ball and quitting cold.

But once he had mastered both his temper and an amazing variety of shots, Jones became a national idol. His adoring public gave him *two* Broadway ticker-tape parades, and the grandest compliment that could be bestowed on six-time women's champion Glenna Collett *(opposite)* was to call her the "Female Bobby Jones."

To celebrate the "Grand Slam," Francis Powers rewrote Grantland Rice's famous passage about the 1924 Notre Dame backfield: "Once again the Four Horsemen of the Apocalypse galloped away together, and their names were Jones, Jones, Jones, Jones." Rice's own tribute, which is excerpted below, was restrained by comparison.

There is no secret connected with Bobby Jones's mastery of the golf world. There are others who have a swing just about as sound, the same determination and the same ability to concentrate. But there is no other who has the all-around combination of these essential elements. This combination happened to meet in one man for the first time in the history of golf.
–Grantland Rice

Looking back over Bobby's matches, you may see crisis after crisis where the least slip in nerve or skill or plain fortune would have spelled blue ruin to Bobby's dearest ambition. Yet at every crisis he stood up to the shot with something which I can define only as inevitability and performed what was needed with all the certainty of a natural phenomenon.
–O. B. Keeler

Golf queen Glenna Collett, a fine natural athlete, suffered a notable upset in 1923 when she lost to Mrs. Caleb Fox, a 60-year-old grandmother.

This Model T, seized in Marfa, Texas, yielded 110 bottles of Mexican hooch—stowed in the spare tire, under the seats and tied to the chassis.

Prohibition

★

AN INVITATION TO LAWLESSNESS

The Noble Experiment

The 1920s were scarcely two weeks old when the United States embarked on one of the maddest follies of a mad decade. On January 16, the 18th Amendment became the law of the land, making liquor, beer and wine illegal throughout the country. With it came the National Prohibition Act (popularly called the Volstead Act, for its primary sponsor), by which the Amendment was to be enforced.

President Hoover called the Amendment "a great social and economic experiment, noble in motive." Noble though it may have been, seldom has law been more flagrantly violated. Not only did Americans continue to manufacture, barter and possess alcohol; they drank more of it. Women, to whom the saloon had been off limits, trooped into Prohibition's invention, the speakeasy, where they consumed quantities of Prohibition's new potion, the cocktail. Moonshining, formerly carried on in the hills by country folk for their own convenience, became big business. So did smuggling; hundreds of ships were anchored three miles off the Atlantic Coast in a line from Maine to Florida, dispensing liquor to anyone who chose to come out by rowboat, skiff or speedboat.

Officers of the law conspired with drinkers to make a travesty of Prohibition. Some of the agents were honest, hardworking men trying to do a thankless job. But Congressman Fiorello H. La Guardia, declaring that it would take a police force of 250,000 to enforce Prohibition in New York City, added sourly that another 200,000 would be required to police the police. In Philadelphia, grafters were said to have pocketed $20 million in three years; in Detroit they hauled in two million dollars a year. In Chicago gangsters held the city in thrall. In Texas, just a few months after the start of Prohibition, a still turning out 130 gallons of whiskey a day was found operating on the farm of Senator Morris Sheppard, one of the authors of the 18th Amendment. In Washington the Prohibition Bureau had the highest turnover of officers of any government agency—some 10,000 men held 3,000 jobs in six years—a fact that elicited from one who remained the rueful comment that the Bureau was running "a training school for bootleggers."

"If you think this country ain't dry," remarked the humorist Will Rogers, "just watch 'em vote; if you think this country ain't wet, just watch 'em drink. You see, when they vote, it's counted, but when they drink, it ain't."

"No person shall, on or after the date when the 18th Amendment to the Constitution of the United States goes into effect, manufacture, sell, barter, transport, import, export, deliver, furnish or possess any intoxicating liquor except as authorized in this act."

Title II, Section 3, National Prohibition Act

A padlock, grim symbol of Prohibition, hangs on the door of a saloon. Lest anyone miss the point, an agent hammers on a sign bearing the sad news.

A floppy overcoat (left) hides two tins of booze strapped to a lady's legs (right). The scene was Detroit, destination of many smugglers from Canada.

Getting Around the Law

American ingenuity, which knows no bounds, had a heyday during Prohibition as people sought ways to tote liquor around without getting arrested. One result was the hip flask; others are shown here. People also hid the stuff in false books and coconut shells, in hot-water bottles strung from their necks and hidden under their clothing, and in garden hose wrapped around their waists, in prams with babies perched on top and in carpenters' aprons with big fat pockets. One man was caught hustling over the International Bridge at Buffalo carrying two boxes of eggs, every one of which had been drained and refilled with liquor. Another tossed some life preservers from a steamship to a friend waiting in a boat in New York Harbor; unhappily he aimed wrong and the whiskey-loaded preservers broke the friend's arm.

Before skirts climbed to the knee, a lady could keep a flask in her garter.

A hollow cane was handy in the street and easy to unplug at the table.

The Saloon Goes Underground

The old-time saloon, bugaboo of the temperance enthusiasts, was the first target of Prohibition enforcers. But it sometimes seemed that for every saloon that closed, a half-dozen underground drinking places—or speakeasies—sprang up. By the summer of 1920, six months after Prohibition began, the speak was an established institution—one that federal agents raided and padlocked in vain, or "protected" for a consideration. By 1925 there were thought to be 100,000 speakeasies in New York City alone. Drinkers said you could get a glass of liquor in any building on 52nd Street between Fifth and Sixth Avenues; the Feds said that 45th Street was the wettest street in the country. Running a speakeasy could net its owner a lot of money. But it took money to make money—one New York proprietor put the cost at $1,370 a month. Of this, $400 was graft to federal Prohibition agents, the police department and the district attorneys. The cop on the beat got another $40 to turn his back whenever beer was delivered. The alternative to making payoffs was to have an elaborate—and expensive—system for concealing the evidence whenever there was a raid. At Manhattan's "21" club there were four alarm buttons at various points in the vestibule (so that if a raider prevented one of them from

Club cards

being pushed, the doorman could reach another). There were also five separate liquor caches, reachable only through secret doors; complicated electric switches opened the doors, and the switches were instantly short-circuited whenever an alarm button was pressed.

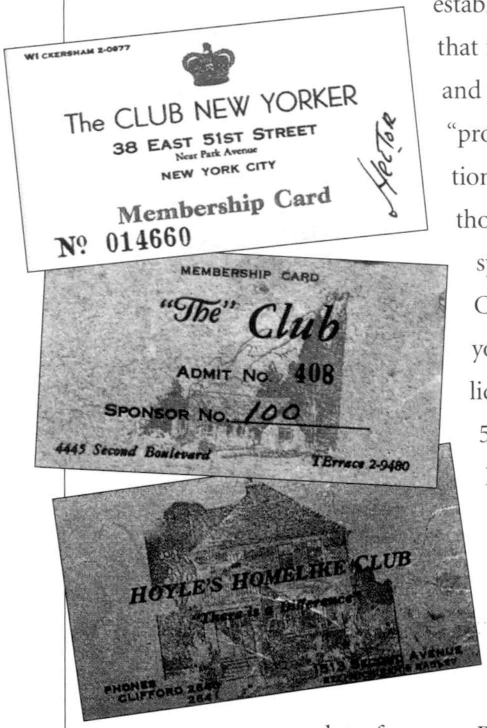

Some speakeasies were known for the quality of their food and liquor; others for the personalities of their owners. Perhaps the most famous speak-owner was Texas Guinan (right), a boisterous blonde who presided over a whole series of rowdy places (when one was shut down she simply moved to another). She plied her customers—whom she wowed with a sassy "Hello, sucker!"—with all they could drink but was said never to have touched the stuff herself. Her earnings during one 10-month period totaled $700,000.

At another extreme was Barney Gallant, equally successful, but as urbane as Texas was noisy. His Club Gallant on Washington Square in Greenwich Village was one of the most posh in New York—partly because Barney, unlike Texas, allowed no drunken rowdiness on his premises. In 1925, with mock solemnity, he promulgated a set of rules for nightclub-goers. An excerpt appears below.

Do not get too friendly with the waiter. His name is neither Charlie nor George. Remember the old adage about familiarity breeding contempt.

Do not ask to play the drums. The drum heads are not as tough as many another head. Besides, it has a tendency to disturb the rhythm.

Make no requests of the leader of the orchestra for the songs of the vintage of 1890. Crooning "Sweet Adeline" was all right for your granddad, but times, alas, have changed.

Pinching the cigarette girl's cheek or asking her to dance with you is decidedly out of order. She is there for the sole purpose of dispensing cigars and cigarettes with a smile that will bring profits to the concessionaire.

Examine your bill when the waiter presents it. Remember even they are human beings and are liable to err—intentionally or otherwise.

Please do not offer to escort the cloakroom girl home. Her husband, who is an ex-prizefighter, is there for that purpose.

Texas Guinan, Queen of the Speak-easies, grins as she boards a paddy wagon. Raided repeatedly, she equably flitted from speak to speak.

Do-It-Yourself Booze

The temperance advocates, who cheered the death of the saloon only to see it replaced by the speakeasy, were in for yet another surprise: certain Americans who had always shied away from the rowdy barroom began to do something they had scarcely done before—drink at home. Half the fun was in making the

---

"It is impossible to tell whether prohibition is a good thing or a bad thing. It has never been enforced in this country. There may not be as much liquor in quantity consumed today as there was before prohibition, but there is just as much alcohol."

Fiorello LaGuardia, in Congressional testimony, 1926

---

booze themselves. For six or seven dollars, a portable still could be purchased in almost any hardware store. If the buyer didn't know how to use it, all he had to do was go to the public library, where he could find, on the open shelves, thousands of books, magazines, even government pamphlets, that described in detail the art of distillation. He could then go home and apply his new knowledge in his own kitchen, using for raw materials prunes, apples, bananas, watermelon, potato peelings, oats or barley.

But there were easier ways. It was a simple matter to get alcohol or ingredients that when mixed together would turn to alcohol, and the manufacturers of scores of products were only too happy to oblige. The vintners of California prospered throughout Prohibition. Under the tutelage of a former Assistant Attorney General, who steered them through the ins and outs of the Prohibition law, they got out a legal product called Vine-Glo—a grape juice which, when put in the cellar and nursed for 60 days, turned into wine that was 15 percent alcohol. Wine-growers even expanded their acreage during Prohibition, from 97,000 in 1919 to 681,000 in 1926, and in 1929 they got a loan from Uncle Sam to expand still more.

Beer was more of a problem, but the brewers, too, found a way. The Volstead Act allowed the manufacture of a concoction containing half of one percent alcohol, called "near beer" (it had been named, according to a current gag, by a poor judge of distance). Nobody wanted near beer—it was tasteless and had no kick. But before long some smart brewer came up with the idea of halting the process of beer-making before there was any alcohol at all, and selling the half-brewed result, called wort, along with a package of yeast that would convey it the rest of the way. What with one thing and another, there was soon so much spirituous beverage being manufactured in the nation's basements, bathrooms and (for all anyone knew to the contrary) bedrooms that an anonymous poet was inspired to write in the New York *World*:

Mother makes brandy from cherries;
Pop distills whiskey and gin;
Sister sells wine from the grapes on our vine—
Good grief, how the money rolls in!

Pictured at right are some of the other devices Americans turned to in an effort to quench their thirst during Prohibition. With the exception of that illegal can of alcohol (*opposite, upper right*) all observed the letter of the law.

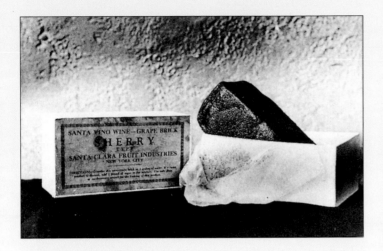

A Brick of Wine

This invention of a New York State vintner, a solid block of grape concentrate about the size of a pound of butter, made a more or less palatable drink when water was added. With it came a circular that solicitously warned the customer what he ought not to do—or else he would have wine, and that would be illegal.

Help for the Patient

Under the Volstead Act, alcohol for medicinal purposes was legal. Doctors prescribed it and druggists dispensed it freely; very soon it was being sold at the rate of a million gallons a year, and the number of "patients" soared. This was one scheme the Prohibition authorities hardly even tried to stop.

Mix and Serve

"The contents of this package," said the label on the can of moonshine alcohol below, "is guaranteed to be distilled from grain only, is free from adulteration." Maybe it was and maybe not; many such products contained wood alcohol. Either way, the buyer added essence of juniper and got a gallon of gin.

Near Beer

Famous brewers like Pabst heeded the law by selling nothing but near beer. But hardly anyone drank it straight. Congressman Fiorello H. La Guardia, an ardent Wet, mixed his with alcoholic malt tonic from the drugstore, and triumphantly posed for his picture, pronouncing the result "delicious!"

Enforcing the Unenforceable

The thankless job of trying to make Prohibition work was assigned to 1,550 federal agents, a mere handful of enforcers sprinkled among hundreds of thousands of violators. The task was simply unmanageable. The Feds were expected to cover 18,700 miles of coastline and inland borders—a confusion of coves and uninhabited woodland that were a smuggler's delight. The harried agents also had to scrutinize hundreds of industries that used alcohol in manufacturing products ranging from shaving cream to Diesel engines. They were expected to track down an ever-expanding crop of stills, a Prohibition growth that flourished like garden weeds. They had to watch the highways for the thousands of beer trucks that rumbled from brewer to speak. They had to sleuth out the devious paths of bootleggers, whose ingenuity never flagged.

For all that, the Feds were regarded with contempt by their fellow countrymen, who had put them in business in the first place. They were the butt of endless jokes, and stories of their corruption, their arrogance, their violence and the manner in which they "protected" speaks and leggers were told in every drinking place. Sometimes the stories were true. Nevertheless, hundreds of Feds did their job honestly and conscientiously. Agents seized half a million gallons of hard liquor and almost five million gallons of beer in 1921; in 1925 they raised their haul to more than a million gallons of liquor and seven million gallons of beer. Considering what they were up against, this was no small feat.

Here and there a Fed made a name for himself, even in that heyday of the scofflaw, for his daring, his ingenuity or even his charm. Two in particular won a niche in Prohibition's Hall of Fame. They were Izzy Einstein and Moe Smith, a pair of zanies from New York's Lower East Side who endeared themselves to the nation for the imagination and good humor with which they went about their jobs. When some years later Izzy wrote his memoirs (an excerpt appears below), he amiably dedicated the book "To the 4,932 persons I arrested, hoping they bear me no grudge for having done my duty." As with many other Prohibition agents, the chief stock in trade of Izzy and Moe were their disguises and the ruses by which they got speakeasy owners—always a wary lot—to tip their hands. To pinch a speak across from Woodlawn Cemetery in New York, Izzy and Moe got themselves up in gravediggers' overalls; to get one in Ithaca they posed as Cornell undergraduates. Another time the roly-poly Izzy (he was 5' 5" and weighed 225 pounds) rounded up 10 other Feds, fitted them out in football suits and daubed them with mud, and then marched them toward a joint near Van Cortlandt Park in the Bronx, where the patrons were sports fans. "In this regalia," wrote Izzy, "we burst into the place announcing with a whoop that now, with the last game of the season over and won, we could break training. Would any saloonkeeper refuse drinks to a bunch of football players in that state of mind? This fellow didn't anyhow. And he discovered that his season was ended too."

Although Izzy and Moe served as Prohibition agents for only five years, the authorities credited them with 20 percent of all Prohibition cases that came to trial in New York City—a phenomenal score for a mere two agents.

A battered Ford proved useful to a couple of other agents and myself in getting us into places as well as getting us around. We'd drive up to a saloon or speakeasy and rush inside asking for the loan of a fountain pen to write a check with. I'd explain that Lizzie was being sold down the river, and my companion, who was to write the check, would insist that the $65 he was paying was a tough bargain because of the condition of the front tires. And I'd come back at him saying I'd guarantee they were good for another thousand miles at the very least.

At any rate the deal would be closed and I'd accept the check; whereupon all differences of opinion as to the car's worth would be forgotten in the desire for a little drink in honor of Lizzie's new owner. And we'd get it. Likewise the fellow who served it to us.

Two federal agents in plainclothes (top) stand before a factory in Massachusetts. In outlandish disguise (above), they set out to raid a speak.

This group of anti-Prohibition demonstrators make their sentiments abundantly clear.

MICHIGAN SQUARE
EL I WANT BEER!
REPEAL
18th COMMANDMEND
DRUG CO.
COUNTRY EGGS
25
40

"Summer shack of a struggling young bootlegger"

King of the Bootleggers

Among the various and sundry suppliers who helped Americans ease that parched feeling during Prohibition, none was more important—and none profited more handsomely—than the bootlegger.

There were small-time 'leggers and big operators. There were bootleggers whose racket was to swipe alcohol from government warehouses, to which some 50 million gallons of liquor manufactured before the start of Prohibition had been consigned for "safekeeping"; at least 20 million gallons of that total had unaccountably disappeared before Prohibition ended. There were bootleggers who stole alcohol from industrial plants, and others who cooked their own in the family basement. Some smuggled the real thing in from abroad, then cut it down with water, sugar and grain alcohol to make three gallons out of every one they had bought; others used whatever came to hand (if the customer was lucky he survived none the worse). One small bootlegger in Brooklyn was asked what the members of his profession used in making bourbon. "Oh," said the man, "they use sugar, garbage, anything they've got. One shiner I know goes around buying up spoiled potatoes from the farmers. He says they ferment nice and quick. Make an awful smell, though."

Bootlegging began on a small scale; it increased mightily as Prohibition wore on. In 1921 federal agents seized just under 96,000 stills and pieces of distilling equipment from bootleggers; in 1925 they took 173,000; in 1930 the seizures reached 282,000. And those figures, of course, do not include the apparatus of thousands of bootleggers who operated without ever getting caught.

Big-time or small-time, gangster or otherwise, bootleggers often became rich, and jokes about their wealth, such as the *Life* cartoon at left, were legion. The most dazzling of them all was George Remus, a bookish intellectual who gave up a flourishing law practice in Chicago to take up the hard liquor trade in Cincinnati. Before getting his law degree Remus had been trained as a pharmacist, and he now turned his early learning to useful account by buying up a dozen Ohio, Kentucky and Missouri distil-

George Remus, titan of the bootleggers, peers wistfully out of a prison cell. He served five sentences for various violations of the liquor laws.

This 60-by-20-foot swimming pool of Italian marble was part of the rococo mansion of bootlegger George Remus in Prince Hill, a suburb of Cincinnati.

In the dining room Remus often placed $100 bills under the plates of his guests.

Mrs. Remus had her own quarters—a boudoir done in the fashion of Louis XVI.

The entrance hall was filled with statuary and flowers from the garden.

leries that the law had allowed to remain in business for the purpose of making medicinal alcohol. So far he was quite within the law. But then he organized an army of 3,000 employees with trucks and siphons, and bade them steal his own product. If his pure booze later ended up in the cutting plants of Chicago and New York, that was not the fault of George Remus. So profitable was the venture that in less than five years he was worth more than five million dollars.

Remus's style of living could have been copied from the *Life* cartoon. His house was a vast gray castle among a blaze of flowering shrubs, set inside an iron fence and graced with every showy luxury imaginable, from a gleaming gold piano to a $125,000 swimming pool. Indoors, no less than out, Remus surrounded himself with sumptuous foliage; his entrance hall was like a Brazilian rain forest. He entertained in a fashion befitting his income and his need for ostentation.

Remus did everything on a grand scale, including lawbreaking. In October 1920, federal Prohibition agents bugged his hotel room and in one day's listening heard him paying off 44 persons, among them other Feds, officers of the Internal Revenue Bureau, warehouse guards and local cops. For this and other lapses he paid fines amounting to $11,000 and did five stints in jail—but none of these cramped his style. On one occasion he traveled to the Atlanta penitentiary in a private club car along with 12 accomplices, who were also prison-bound; their every wish was seen to by a private staff of waiters who served a lavish array of food and drink. They chugged out of the Cincinnati station with the cheers of 500 well-wishers ringing in their ears. On arrival, Remus lived nearly as well as he had at home. He ate his meals at the home of the prison chaplain and equipped his cell with maid service—and, his passion, fresh flowers every day.

Meanwhile, back in Cincinnati, his dark-eyed wife, Imogene, kept up appearances, her spirits buoyed by the attentions of one Franklin L. Dodge, who happened to be the Fed who had got Remus thrown into the clink. When after 19 months the prisoner was about to be sprung, Imogene filed for divorce; Remus filed a countersuit, charging that Imogene had conspired with Dodge to get him framed. Neither case ever got to court, for one morning Remus followed his wife on a ride through the city park, caught up and shot her in the stomach. Tried for the shooting, Remus was acquitted on grounds of temporary insanity, and then, a stylist to the end, he repaired to the local jailhouse, where rumor had it he threw a magnificent party for an assortment of friends—and 12 jurors.

Racketeering Comes of Age

Of all the evils to come out of Prohibition, by far the worst was the explosive growth of big-time crime. Gangsters were nothing new (as the Drys were quick to point out); they had flourished long before Prohibition, running saloons, bawdyhouses and gambling joints, and doing dirty work for employers and workers alike in labor disputes. But when the gangsters took over bootlegging—and what better racket to grab?—they opened a chapter in history that made the violence of frontier days look like child's play.

Every city had its gangs and gang leaders. New York had half a dozen, among them two led by thugs named Dutch Schultz and Owney Madden; Philadelphia had its Maxie Hoff; Kansas City had one Solly Weissman; and Detroit, a major entry point for smugglers, had an outfit known as the Purple Gang. But queen of them all was Chicago, a luckless city whose name became a synonym for violence, thuggery and mass murder.

Prohibition was scarcely born before the gangs began to capitalize on it. They organized their minions into alky cookers and rum runners. They bought out hundreds of breweries, and transported the beer in armored trucks across the U.S. highways. They stationed armed men on the borders to hijack other dealers' consignments. They set up cutting plants, where genuine liquor was adulterated. They swooped on the speakeasies, making the owners clearly understand whom they had to buy their booze from.

The evil genius of all gangsterdom was Al Capone, first summoned to Chicago at 23 by Johnny Torrio, who was at the time boss of the Windy City's underworld. Capone came out from New York, where he had served his apprenticeship in the notorious Five Points ring in Brooklyn. When he arrived in Chicago, a scar-faced rookie carrying the family Bible, he was enrolled as Torrio's lieu-tenant. In a few years he had sewn up all rackets in the town of Cicero, a suburb west of Chicago.

By the time Torrio abdicated leadership of the rackets and ceded the crown to him in 1925, Capone had an army of 700 men to do his bidding; before the end of the decade he controlled all 10,000 speakeasies in Chicago and was said to be ruling the entire bootlegging business from Canada to Florida. He gave his orders from an armored office that took up a whole floor of Chicago's Hawthorne Hotel, and he rode about in an armored limousine, preceded by one armed car a block ahead of him and followed by another close behind.

He needed the protection. During the racketeers' reign of terror, Chicago suffered upwards of 400 gang murders a year. Rival gangs, named for their leaders—the Aiellos, the Gennas, the O'Banions and several dozen others—vied with the master's own troops in the ingenuity of their murder schemes.

Those murders came to a shocking climax on Valentine's Day in 1929, when Capone sent his men after the O'Banions. Dion O'Banion, besides having a take in the beer racket, had run a flower shop that supplied the blooms for a market he helped create—felled gangsters were treated to funerals that set records of extravagance in tonnage of flowers, ornate coffins and milling crowds. O'Banion himself had been killed five years before, but his followers, led now by Bugs Moran, were still avenging his death. When Capone had had enough of that, he ordered his henchman Machine Gun Jack McGurn to do the O'Banions in for good, a task that Jack discharged with an imaginativeness that was unusual even in that innovative era. He dispatched a band of his cronies, fitted out in police uniforms, to a garage where seven of O'Banion's men were waiting for a haul of hijacked hooch. The phony cops entered the garage on the pretext that they were making a raid and proceeded to cut down the seven in one sweeping blast of machine-gun fire. Then they spirited themselves off in a waiting Cadillac that the authorities never caught up with in the mid-morning traffic.

Chief of Capone's gunners, Machine Gun Jack McGurn masterminded a massacre on Valentine's Day in 1929.

A longtime ruler of brothels and opium dens, Big Jim Colosimo was Chicago's first Prohibition gang chief.

"I'm getting out," said Johnny Torrio to Capone after rivals gunned him down.

Joe Saltis was a leader of Chicago's West Side—until he threatened "them damn Sicilians."

"I'll kill you for this," said surly Earl Weiss to the photographer who took this picture.

Al Capone's vassals went off on their various assignments crying, "All for Al, Al for All!"

George Bugs Moran was an archrival of Capone—until his gang fell in the Valentine's Day massacre.

Pickpocket and safe-cracker, Dion O'Banion hit it big with Torrio and soon bossed the North Side.

William O'Donnell and his brother Myles, "guerillas of the bootleg war," dared invade Capone's Cicero.

A Dallas newsstand offers a variety of journals.

A Lively Press

★

THE BIRTH OF THE TABLOIDS

The Detective Story Magazine

Atlantic Monthly

New Vigor in the Public Print

"He was the editor of the tabloid 'newspaper' but he loved his children. So he told them he was a burglar."

College Humor, 1927

Their appetites for news whetted by a world war, their leisure augmented by the eight-hour day, their literacy rate climbing, Americans turned hungrily to the printed word. The newspapers gave them a rich and varied diet. From *The New York Times* they got top-notch foreign correspondence. In the New York *World* they could read Franklin P. Adams, Heywood Broun and other superlatively witty columnists. The exposé of evildoing in high places became the mark of many a good paper: the *St. Louis Post-Dispatch* forced an allegedly corrupt federal judge to resign; the *Indianapolis Times* exposed Indiana's Ku Klux Klan leader as a murderer. Newspaper circulation boomed; the total for the nation was about 25 million when the decade started and about 40 million at its close. The first of the tabloids arrived in 1919, with the most lurid news coverage the country had ever known;

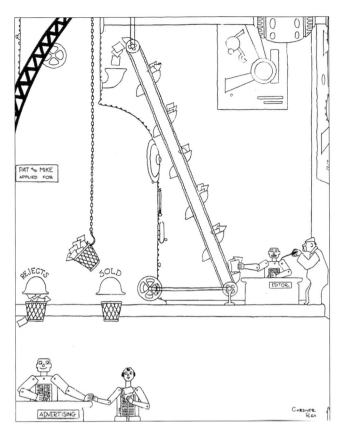

Popular Mechanics

The New Yorker

the competition shook the old business to its roots.

Magazines, meanwhile, experienced an unprecedented boom. While *The Saturday Evening Post, Collier's, National Geographic, Literary Digest* and other old mass market giants reached circulation peaks, new magazines began challenging the established order with their candor and iconoclasm. The *American Mercury*, founded in 1924 and edited by curmudgeons H. L. Mencken (*page 153*) and George Jean Nathan, lambasted Rotarians, Babbitts, Fundamentalists and the rest of what Mencken called the "booboisie." *Time*, the first of the news magazines, started in 1923. The *New Yorker*, launched in 1925, tackled American life with a deft, wicked, penetrating wit. Several old-timers were at the forefront of this vigorous journalism: the *Forum* sought out debates on troubling issues and staid old *Scribner's*

was banned in Boston for running Ernest Hemingway's *A Farewell to Arms* as a serial.

All was not highbrow, however; by 1926, Bernarr Macfadden's *True Story Magazine* (founded in 1919) was titillating a readership of nearly two million with tales of love among the shopgirls; a host of competing confession magazines sprang up in its wake.

The magazines poked fun at everything—including other magazines. To the *New Yorker*'s condescending proclamation that it was not being published "for the old lady in Dubuque," *Time* commented loftily: "There is no provincialism so blatant as that of the metropolitan who lacks urbanity." In 1929 a series of cartoons in the humorous weekly *Life*, some of which are reproduced above, satirized, with sharp perception, a score of *Life*'s competitors.

The Lurid
Little Journals

In the Style of the 20s

The nine pages that follow have been made up to resemble the tabloids of the era. The news stories (with minor adaptations) are real and so are the headlines; in some cases the headlines may have come from one paper, the pictures from another. The stories deal with some of the decade's most famous events—famous not necessarily because they were important, but because they lent themselves to the sensationalism that was the hallmark of the tabs. The facing picture, for example, shows the execution of Ruth Snyder, a Long Island housewife who persuaded her lover to help kill her husband; both went to the electric chair in January 1928. To scoop its rivals on the execution, the New York Daily News smuggled an out-of-town (and therefore unfamiliar) photographer into the death chamber. His camera was strapped to his leg; at the appropriate moment, he crossed one knee over the other, uncovering the lens, and squeezed a bulb in his pocket to snap the shutter.

This picture of husband-killer Ruth Snyder at the moment of her electrocution was the most famous tabloid photo of the decade.

The raffish '20s produced a special kind of newspaper to match the spirit of the times. The tabloids were only half the standard newspaper size, which made them easier to handle on crowded subway trains, especially in New York, where most of them were published. But it was content, rather than size, that really marked them. Racily written, lavishly illustrated, sensationally headlined, the tabloids served up a daily dish of sex and violence that pulled in readers by the hundreds of thousands. The first of these papers, the New York *Daily News,* was launched in June 1919; five years later it had the nation's highest newspaper circulation— about three quarters of a million. Such success was not allowed to go unchallenged. In June 1924 the New York *Daily Mirror* was started by William Randolph Hearst; three months later Bernarr Macfadden, a physical-culturist and exponent of clean living, gave the masses the most lurid paper of all, the *Evening Graphic,* soon nicknamed the Pornographic.

The tabs introduced sensationalism on a scale never before known—not only in New York but also in other cities where newspapers copied the tabloids' approach, if not always their size. They invented a new headline lexicon ("love nests," "torch murders," "sugar daddies," "heart balm"); they pioneered the development of the gossip columnist; and they covered the news with unprecedented aggressiveness.

When sensations were lacking, the tabs thought nothing of creating them; in 1926 the *Daily Mirror* resurrected the four-year-old Hall-Mills murder case, nominated a murderer and actually forced the case to a trial before running out of steam. When dramatic pictures were not available some papers manufactured their own; the *Graphic's* chief stock in trade was the faked picture, or composograph—a posed photograph with the faces of news figures superimposed on it. At one point the *Graphic's* heedless news tactics left the paper facing libel suits totaling $12 million.

All this was accompanied by pious lip service to the morality of the time. Editorials preached that crime did not pay; it didn't for criminals, but it did for the tabs. The photo of Ruth Snyder on the facing page boosted the *News's* circulation by one million; the electrocution of anarchists Sacco and Vanzetti was worth an extra 185,000 copies; mail robber Gerald Chapman's hanging increased sales by 110,000. "Some convict was executed at Sing Sing last night," said Macfadden one day to his managing editor. "Run a full-page picture of his face and on it use a two-word headline, two inches high: 'ROASTED ALIVE.'"

Eventually the tabloids would grow more restrained, but during the decade they placed an indelible stamp on American journalism.

DEATH IN THE CHAIR

© NEW YORK "DAILY NEWS"

OUR AIMEE IS BACK!!

The "Kidnaping" of Aimee

Even in a time of flamboyant personalities, Aimee Semple McPherson was outstanding. A comely, showbiz-minded Hollywood evangelist, Aimee failed to return from a California beach excursion on May 18, 1926; her disappearance created a national sensation. After 37 days she stumbled out of the desert in Arizona, saying she had escaped from kidnapers. Reporters flocked to the scene, among them the Los Angeles Examiner's sob sister, Marjorie Driscoll, who wrote the tearjerker excerpted at right. Then suspicious people began asking questions. Why did Aimee's clothes show no sign of her ordeal? Why hadn't she been parched after her long desert walk? Soon the papers that had whipped up sympathy for Mrs. McPherson were implying that, far from suffering, she had been enjoying a month-long idyll with a boyfriend. The story finally dropped off the front pages, but while it lasted it was an editor's dream.

AIMEE SEMPLE McPHERSON (shown in her robes in insert) gets an uproarious welcome from 30,000 Angelenos, more than turned out to see visiting Presidents Taft or Wilson, as she returns home after her kidnaping. Later, while disciples strewed flowers in her path, Aimee was carried from her special railroad car in a wicker chair laced with roses and carnations.

Aimee's Tears of Joy Greet Beloved Ones

Douglas, Ariz., June 24—Beyond spoken words, beyond anything but inarticulate sobs and an embrace that clung as if it would never let go was the reunion this morning of Aimee Semple McPherson and her mother, Mrs. Minnie Kennedy. A mother held her girl close to her again; her girl, given up for dead.

They met in the little white room of the Calumet Hospital, a room banked with flowers sent by the people of Douglas. Mrs. Kennedy came, hair running, up the steps of the hospital to the room where Aimee was lying. A privileged few followed her to the threshold and waited in a silence that throbbed with joy and tears.

A PASSIONATE EMBRACE

The tired worn woman in the bed turned a glorified face toward the door. She stretched out her arms. The silken sleeves of the pink dressing gown fell back and showed cruel bruises on her wrists. Straight to these waiting arms went the mother. They held her close, close in a passionate embrace. To those who waited at the door came little broken sobs, inarticulate caresses. For long minutes the two clung to each other. Mrs. McPherson's arm tightened around her mother's neck, quivered. It held fast. There was no sound except broken whispers as mother and daughter wept together.

Roberta and Rolf, Mrs. McPherson's children, waited eagerly. Roberta's lips trembled a little. Rolf stood straight and steady, his face grave beyond his years. Then Mrs. Kennedy stepped back and Roberta and Rolf ran forward to feel their mother's arms about them again.

When that first sacred moment ended, Mrs. McPherson looked at the men and women who pressed forward to stand about her bed. Her lips quivered, her throat throbbed with a joy that was near to tears. "Oh, you dear people, you dear people," she whispered.

AN EMOTIONAL MOMENT

Mrs. McPherson caught sight of a reporter from the Examiner whom she had known. "Come here," she called. "I want to see you." Her arms were like tense bands of steel, trembling but strong around my shoulders. I could feel the quick shudders that ran through her body, the throbbing of nerve and muscle. "Oh, my dear, aren't you glad for me?" she whispered as her lips clung in a long kiss. "It's so good, so wonderful."

Joy and excitement held Mrs. McPherson up through the meeting, through the gentle questioning of Captain Cline and Ryan. It was not until her tired body could stand no more that she fainted quietly among the flowers and the pretty nurses sent the crowd away.

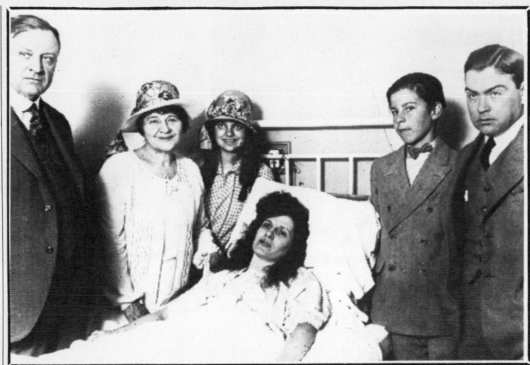

RECOVERING IN THE HOSPITAL, Aimee is visited by mother and children, Roberta and Rolf.

Evangelist Relives Kidnaping

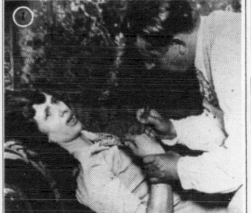

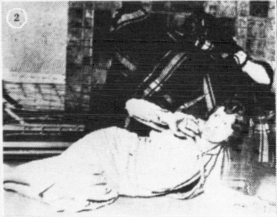

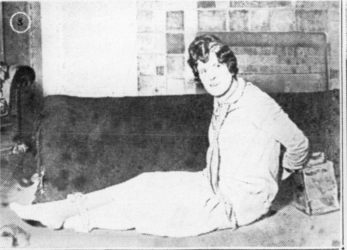

RE-ENACTING THE KIDNAPING, Aimee demonstrates how (1) her fingers were burned by a cigar wielded by one of her abductors (2) the kidnapers swathed her in blankets (3) she was then tied up and (4) she managed to escape before struggling across the desert to safety.

Struggle to Free Collins

EXPLORER ENTOMBED IN UNDERGROUND PASSAGE

Cave City, Ky., Feb. 2—Floyd Collins is suffering torture almost beyond description. Until I went inside myself I wondered why someone couldn't do something quick, but I found out why.

The passageway is about five feet in diameter. I had to squirm like a snake. Water covers almost every inch of the ground. Every moment it got colder. After going about ninety feet I reached a small compartment, slightly larger than the rest of the channel. I slid down an eight-foot drop and, a moment later, saw Collins.

My flashlight revealed a face on which is written suffering of many long hours, because Collins has been in agony every conscious moment since he was trapped. I saw the purple of his lips, the pallor on his face, and realized that something must be done before long if this man is

SIGHTSEERS gather outside the Kentucky cave in which explorer Floyd Collins lies trapped.

to live. Before I could see his face, however, I was forced to raise a small piece of oil cloth covering it.

"Put it back," he said. "Put it back—the water!"

Then I noticed a small drip-drip-drip from above. Each drop struck Collins' face. The first hours he didn't mind, but the constant dripping almost drove him insane. His brother Homer had taken the oil cloth to him earlier in the day.

NEVER WITHOUT PAIN

Collins' foot, held by a six-ton rock in a natural crevice, is never without pain. I tried to squirm over Collins' body to reach the rock, until he begged me to get off. "It hurts—hurts awful," he said. Collins is lying on his back, resting more on the left side. His two arms are held fast in the crevice beside his body, so that he really is in a natural straight-jacket.

I was followed by Homer Collins, brother of the victim, and Guy Turner. Homer Collins had brought with him some body harness to place around his brother, and we finally succeeded in putting it on him. The prisoner helped by turning as much as possible and finally we were ready to haul on the rope attached to Collins. We pulled as much as we could and estimated we moved the prisoner five inches. All of us were on the point of collapse and after a short time our strength failed.

We couldn't do any more. We left near his head a lantern. The tiny light it throws may bring some bit of consolation.

Sand Cave, Cave City, Ky., Feb. 3—Late this afternoon it was decided that Collins might be rescued by drilling through the side of a hill and tunneling through behind him. The work was started by seven drillers but was halted after a short time. It was feared that the vibration would dislodge huge rocks above Collins and crush him to death.

TOMB SEALING ITSELF

Everett Maddox volunteered today to go back into the dangerous tunnel and bathe the victim's face. Maddox went in at 9:45 o'clock this morning with towel and water. Silently he turned the face of the prisoner as he bathed it. He brushed back the hair from the sunken eyes. As he worked there in the clammy chamber, Maddox read on the face a story of agony and suffering and despair. Earth, using the corpse as bait, is waiting to crush anyone daring enough to venture in. The tomb is sealing itself in collapse. In the opinion of experts, a person going in stands but a small chance to return. Collins' body is in sight but is farther out of reach than ever.

The Death of Floyd Collins

Seeking a cavern to attract tourist trade, Floyd Collins, a 30-year-old Kentuckian, went exploring one day in 1925 in the underground honeycomb near Mammoth Cave. Suddenly a boulder shifted, fell across his ankle and trapped him in a narrow passage 126 feet from the surface. A neighbor boy found him there a day later and ran for help. Among the 150 reporters who turned up at the scene was 21-year-old William "Skeets" Miller of the Louisville Courier-Journal. Five times Miller—alone among all the newsmen—descended into the dark tunnel to talk to Collins and to try to help him. But all efforts to rescue the trapped man failed, and while the nation watched in fascination and horror, Collins died of exposure. During the 18 days the story lasted, the cave site became the scene of a fantastic carnival. Mobs of sightseers hampered rescue efforts; Collins's neighbors sold hamburgers for a quarter and rented cots for three dollars a night. The cave was finally sealed off with Collins's body still in it. Miller won a Pulitzer Prize for his reports, which are excerpted here.

Last Try to Aid Cave Victim

FLOYD COLLINS

RESCUERS prepare to lower a miner into a shaft in the ground, dug in an effort to find a new cavern opening that will give access to Floyd Collins' cave.

BROTHER of the trapped man, Homer Collins watches anxiously at the mouth of the cave, along with the family dog.

PARENTS of Floyd Collins, Mr. and Mrs. Lee Collins (seated at center), attend the funeral of their son.

Peaches Says 'I Longed for a Child'

ON THE HONEYMOON, says Peaches, Daddy got dressed up like a sheik, brought along his pet goose, and barked at his bride.

Daddy and Peaches

The saga of Daddy and Peaches, the December-May romance of a 51-year-old New York millionaire and a 15-year-old schoolgirl, wedded in 1926 after a three-month courtship, would probably have gone its ordinary way had it not been for the New York Evening Graphic. But when realtor Edward "Daddy" Browning and plump Frances "Peaches" Browning split up after a half year of marriage, the Graphic joyously moved in. Peaches, anxious to tell all, was signed up for her exclusive story. Then, while she belabored Daddy in one column, the paper enticed Browning into answering in another. The Graphic employed its famous composograph (above) to give the sad tale a display befitting its moral. When the Graphic editors were arrested on a complaint by the Society for the Suppression of Vice, the paper ran this story, too. Why not? It all helped to build up circulation.

WHY I LEFT DADDY BROWNING

By Frances Heenan Browning

My dream of love has turned into a hideous, revolting nightmare. I had to run away. My health, my future and my self-respect were at stake. My nerves were shattered. But can I forget? When I think of the terrible hours I spent—in the night. When I think of the peculiar look in his eye, sometimes! When I think of what happened in his moments of abandon. Anything is better than the horrors of those haunting days and nights.

I am a normal girl with the instincts for love, wifehood and motherhood that every girl has. Mr. Browning did not satisfy those instincts. Mr. Browning declares: "Mrs. Heenan slept in Mrs. Browning's room. To even as much as whisper to my wife, I had to awaken Mrs. Heenan." That is not true. Mother didn't always sleep in the same room. My mother wasn't with us when we went on our honeymoon motor trip. We were quite alone in the hotels where we stopped! I really wish now that my mother had been with me every minute. I would have been a very different girl now.

A FEAR OF CONVULSIONS

I never refused to have a baby. I never said I didn't want one. And Mr. Browning knows that is true! I cried and cried last night when I read his statement saying all sorts of things about me. My mother was afraid I would have another one of those convulsions like I used to have while I was living with him.

There has been a lot of talk about why I married Mr. Brown-

Daddy:'Peaches Wife in Name Only'

THE BROWNINGS AT HOME shared their love nest with Peaches' Mama. Daddy says Mama was always around and spoiled the fun.

DADDY AND PEACHES kiss for the camera as they celebrate her 16th birthday. Peaches is holding his present—a $10,000 check. Nowadays she says Daddy did it for the publicity but was really stingy.

ing and why Mr. Browning married me. MR. BROWNING MARRIED ME TO PROTECT HIMSELF. Certain police authorities told my mother and me that an investigation was about to be started into Mr. Browning's experiences with little girls. His marriage to me halted that investigation. MY HAPPINESS, MY FUTURE, EVERYTHING I HAD, WAS SACRIFICED ON THE ALTAR OF HIS SELFISHNESS!

Nothing humiliated me more than Mr. Browning's craving for publicity. It is an overwhelming obsession with him. He wanted the newspaper men to know everything about us—what I wore, the color of my nighties, the size of our bed.

A lot of people say I married Mr. Browning for his money. That is absolutely false. Money was the last thing in my mind when I met him. I would have given up every nice dress I ever had to have been spared the

moment of torture when Mr. Browning would come lumbering into our bedroom and growl

Daddy Replies!

Oct. 12, 1926—In an astonishing interview, Edward West Browning, self-anointed "High Priest of the Daddy Cult," stood last night in his pulpit of business and there, amid the ruins of his Temple of Love, revealed to the world through the GRAPHIC the most intimate details of his married life with Peaches Heenan. "I wanted, oh how I longed for a CHILD OF MY OWN," he sobbed out in his heart anguish. Here is his story:

"Peaches did not sleep with me. From the very first night she has always slept with her mother. My marriage was IN NAME only. From our very wedding night Peaches has denied me my rights as a husband. I had hoped to play on the harp of celestial raptures. I thought I

"Woof! Woof!" like a bear in my ear. I was so frightened I went into a sort of swoon.

would be surrounded by the angels of love. Gnomes alone fluttered about. I don't want to say anything unkind, and even now I won't call my mother-in-law names, but she proved to be no dove of peace. I want Peaches back. I want to be a father. Peaches needs me and my care. I won't say she suffers from epilepsy, but she is a victim of something very close to epileptic fits, she rolls her eyes and froths at the mouth. In her story she charges that mine was a strange and weird love, and intimates that I have lost my virility. I am willing to submit to examination by any reputable group of physicians and they will prove that I am as virile and potent as a youth of 20."

CONFESS THRILL MURDER OF BOY

"BOBBY" FRANKS, 14

THE SEARCH FOR EVIDENCE takes investigators to Hesseville, Ind., just across the state line from Chicago. After burning Bobby's clothes in the furnace of Loeb's home, the murderers buried his belt-buckle, shoes and jewelry, all non-combustible, in the country. Loeb's father, at far right wearing a gray coat, helped in the search.

The Leopold-Loeb Case

The tabloids had their standard way of handling a big story. When one didn't fit the mold—no matter; they covered it the same way. In 1924 two wealthy Chicago college boys, Nathan Leopold and Richard Loeb, went on trial for the "thrill" murder of 14-year-old Bobby Franks. The great attorney Clarence Darrow, attracted in part by the apparent hopelessness of the case, conducted the defense. In the process he charted new legal grounds based on the psychoanalytic doctrines of Sigmund Freud. Darrow did not deny that Leopold and Loeb had committed the murder; he held that they were so emotionally disturbed that they could not be held responsible for their actions. Although this unorthodox view persuaded the court, it left the newspapers unmoved. Their stories, exemplified by the New York Daily News accounts excerpted here, followed standard tabloid techniques. They included a report that Darrow was to receive a million dollars for his labors. Actually, he got only $30,000.

Millionaires' Sons Leopold, Loeb Justify Revolting Crime as Scientific

Chicago, May 30—"We are near a solution of the Robert Franks slaying" was the word from the prosecuting attorney's office as the shadow of the great mystery fell heavily upon Richard Loeb, son of the millionaire vice president of Sears Roebuck and Co., and Nathan Leopold Jr., also the son of a millionaire, an honor student, ornithologist, linguist, radical and a leading member of the so-called Intelligentsia, which has small regard for the laws and ethics of this or any other country.

Chicago, May 31—Nathan Leopold Jr., 19 and Richard Loeb, also 19, today confessed to the murder of Robert Franks.

Chicago, June 1 —"Anything is justifiable in the interests of science," said Nathan Leopold, Jr., one of the murderers of fourteen-year-old Bobby Franks.

"It is no crime to use a human being in the interest of scientific research. It is no more than impaling a beetle on a pin."

"I'll admit we're in Dutch," said Richard Loeb, who helped slay the boy.

The cold-blooded attitude of the young murderers amazes those with whom they have come in contact. Today they went in automobiles, under guard of a squad of detectives, and re-enacted the entire crime.

They drove to the point where the boy was picked up from the street, struck over the head with a padded chisel, smothered in a robe and a cloth thrust into his mouth.

At the swamp the young murderers showed how Loeb had remained in the hired car while Leopold carried the nude body of the boy to a large culvert and thrust it into the opening.

Chicago, June 5—Indictments were voted by the grand jury tonight charging Nathan F. Leopold, Jr. and Richard Loeb with the murder of Robert Franks.

State's Attorney Crowe announced with the departure of the grand jurors that everything had been presented, except only Loeb's confession, which, he said, differed but slightly from Leopold's.

They disagreed, the prosecutor said, on which one evolved the scheme that led to their present plight; which first suggested committing murder for sport, or which was driving the automobile, and as to which actually killed Robert.

Each said the other did the suggesting and the killing, each claiming to have been driving when Robert was slain.

Chicago, June 8—When Leopold and Loeb go on trial shortly, a court room drama unique in criminal history will be staged. The court room itself will become a clinic. There will be revealed, opened, probed and torn to shreds, a new factor in crime —the "campus mind."

Such are the plans of Clarence Darrow. It is said Darrow alone will receive $1 million in excess of his fee if he succeeds in saving the two boys. College students are to be summoned to the witness stand in the startling plan to introduce the jury to the "campus mind" which, it is said, Darrow will claim has become a product of the new theories of ultra-modern college education.

Chicago, Sept. 10—Leopold and Loeb were today sentenced to the penitentiary for life. Leopold showed no sign of emotion. Loeb blinked his eyes.

LEOPOLD AND LOEB (at right) enter Joliet Penitentiary.

THE FATEFUL TYPEWRITER on which Leopold wrote to Bobby's father demanding $10,000 was tossed into a lagoon by the criminals. They never got the money; the boy's body was found before it could be delivered. The portable was recovered by a diver.

A TENSE MOMENT IN COURT

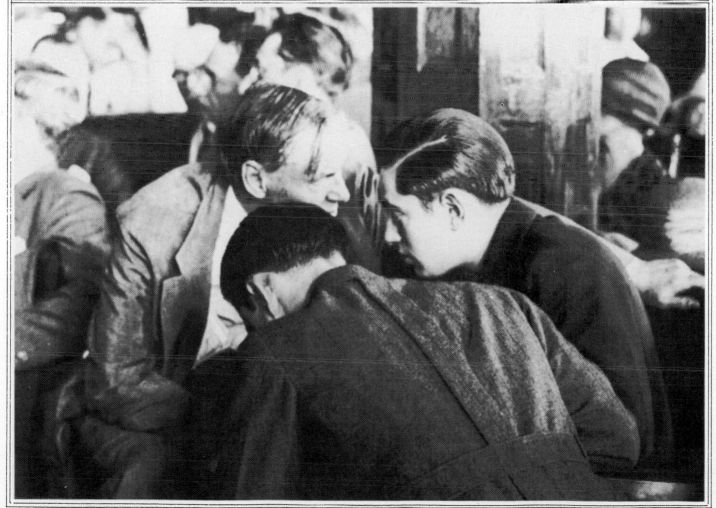

DEFENSE COUNSEL Clarence Darrow discusses a point of law with Loeb (back to camera) and Leopold during the murder trial.

Valentino Poisoned? BROADWAY HEARS! DOCTORS DENY!

New York, Aug. 23—Rudolph Valentino, the great sheik of the movies, a pale and wasted figure of a man, sighed a little and was still. Rudy died in his sleep. His breath ceased at 12:30.

Millions of women had known and loved him during his short, colorful life. Women had stood out in the rain and the cold and blazing heat to see him. He was dead—and there had been no woman there to say goodbye, no woman to stroke his sleek, black hair, or hold his head, or close his eyes with a kiss. Jean Acker, his first wife, had called up the hospital but she never visited him. Natacha Rambova sent no word. Pola Negri is in Hollywood. She fainted yesterday when she heard the news, it is said.

Even the nurses had gone—and there were only men in the room. He could laugh at that Chicago editorial writer now, the one who had laughed at his slave bracelets and his powder puffs. He was a he-man, dying in the presence of he-man friends.

New York, Aug. 24—There flew along Broadway yesterday sinister reports that Rudolph Valentino came to his death by arsenic poisoning. Circumstantial stories told of both jealousy and revenge as the supposed motives. Immediately upon the heels of the first report Dr. William B. Rawles of Polyclinic Hospital denied formally that Valentino had been poisoned.

New York, Aug. 24—In life Rudolph Valentino drew excited, romance-hungry crowds. In death he draws a mob. Rudy lay in his silver bronze coffin, a $10,000 coffin with an unbreakable glass over his face. The crowd would not be patient and would not wait to see him. They crashed in through a plate glass window, carrying the police with them. They went through it with an angry roar, falling, screaming, hitting out with their fists, stepping on those in their way. Horses trampled some of them. Others fainted. From 75 to 100 were hurt. But nothing could keep them away. There went a girl in her stocking feet, weeping hysterically, soaked to the skin, her new hat a ruin. She was crying: "I must see him! I must see him."

POLICE CHARGE CROWD

As the news spread that Rudy was to lie in state the crowd began to grow. There were the police charging the crowd, the iron hoofs going click-clack, click-clack on the wet cement, and women screamed and laughed and ran out of the way, and then ran back again. The policemen use their fists, grab hats, hurl them away, whirl their horses around. Women faint. Women scream. Women fight to get in.

"Get in line." The crowd was milling everywhere, but finally it got itself into a long, unwieldy, savage and impatient line. A line 10 blocks long. A line of um-

brellas glistening with the rain.

It had been the intention to keep the body on view, but this was changed. Because of the irreverence. Because of the excitement. Because of the rioting and the laughter and the screams. Because some women coming out after the last look at the waxen face of the actor had laughed profanely. It was learned, too, that men were making a business of selling their places in the lines. Ghouls! Making a dollar or two by squeezing in here, moving up, and selling out. Other men were selling umbrellas, sandwiches, rubbers.

All day long letters came into the DAILY MIRROR, letters enclosing poems, letters extolling Rudy. This is just one of them, the letter of an aged woman who signs herself Ruthie Rose Burr:

"So much has been said and written in eulogy of Rudolph Valentino. May I, a three score and ten grandmother, offer my reason I felt for that estimable gentleman. It is a pity that one who so ably supplied to romance-starved women the picturesque and beautiful side of life should be called out. He was the 'wonderful lover' and the finished portrayer of the exquisite fop, and yet giving no impression of effeminacy. I know of no other actor quite so elegant. Until my final curtain I shall miss him."

Mourning The Sheik

On August 23, 1926, the movie actor Rudolph Valentino, 31, died in a Manhattan hospital. In less than five years, the sleek Valentino had established himself as king of the cinema lovers—"catnip to women," H. L. Mencken called him. Valentino's death set off an epidemic of female hysteria. In London a dancer swallowed poison. In New York a housewife drank iodine and shot herself twice before sinking down on a pile of his photographs. Newspapers and press agents fanned the fever. Film flacks hired 20 women to weep at the funeral parlor; they attracted 30,000 unruly mourners who lined up for hours for a one-second glimpse of "The Sheik." When the New York Evening Graphic ran a composograph depicting the Great Lover meeting his compatriot Enrico Caruso in heaven, circulation rose by 100,000. The News cooked up a fake poison story (above), and the Daily Mirror gave away pictures of The Sheik. These two papers ran the liveliest accounts of the event, excerpted here.

Women Trampled at Sheik's Bier

RUDY'S BODY lies in state as fan Eva Miller prays by the bier. His manager, fearing that ghoulish visitors might seek souvenirs, later had the casket sealed so that only Rudy's face showed.

A LAST GLIMPSE of Rudy attracts 100,000 mourners in two days.

NEW YORK'S FINEST control a sorrowing crowd in the rain.

POLA NEGRI leaves the funeral parlor after saying a farewell to her beloved. Pola said she and Rudy were planning to wed.

Notables

★

A GALLERY OF GREATS

THANATOPSIS PLEASUR

Literary figures and friends sit down to poker (key, page 146).

ND INSIDE STRAIGHT CLUB

"The inferior man must find himself superiors, that he may marvel at his political equality with them."

H. L. Mencken

This is a key to the drawing on the preceding spread, which was done by cartoonist Will Cotton in 1929: 1. humorist Dorothy Parker; 2. columnist Franklin P. Adams; 3. banker Henry Wise Miller; 4. socialite Gerald Brooks; 5. publisher Raoul Fleischmann; 6. playwright George S. Kaufman; 7. manufacturer Paul Hyde Bonner; 8. humorist Robert Benchley; 9. columnist Heywood Broun; 10. writer Alexander Woollcott; 11. novelist Alice Duer Miller; 12. comedian Harpo Marx; 13. reporter George Backer; 14. songwriter Irving Berlin; 15. editor Harold Ross ; 16. Mrs. George S. Kaufman; 17. editor Herbert Bayard Swope; 18. stage star Joyce Barbour; 19. theatrical producer Crosby Gaige.

A Nation of Hero Worshipers

In the jovial mood of the 1920s, Americans held up for public inspection and applause a new creature: the celebrity, the big name in the news, whose most trivial comings and goings were recorded by the press in much the same way that the village eccentric on Main Street is watched by busybodies peering through scrim curtains.

The celebrities might be in any walk of life—politics, adventure, the arts or letters—so long as what they were doing, or how they did it, was sufficiently voguish or offbeat to get the public's attention. The celebrity might be a natural curiosity by virtue of his office, like the President, or someone brought to renown by self-promotion, like a stunt man; or someone whose occupation merited a shining place in lights or in print, like an actor or a writer. Either way, the newspapers and the magazines put the celebrities' names and faces, their every word and deed, before the public eye, in intimate, gossipy fashion.

Some celebrities merely created hoopla; others were at the forefront of the intellectual movement that was bringing American letters of age. The capital of the movement was New York, the Mecca to which aspiring youth of talent flocked like pilgrims. Some of these found acclaim alone; others found it in groups. Among the latter, one of the most widely quoted was a coterie known as the Round Table, a brilliant collection of writers and actors who regularly lunched at the Algonquin Hotel on West 44th Street.

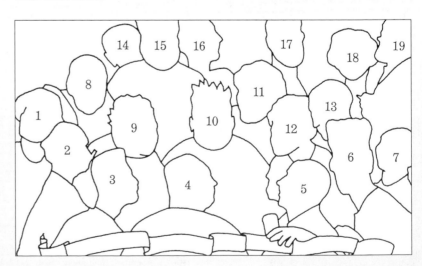

Robert Benchley

Harold Ross

Alexander Woollcott

Dorothy Parker

George S. Kaufman

The Round Table had an impromptu beginning; its earliest members were three droll youths, Robert Benchley *(page 147)*, Dorothy Parker *(opposite, lower left)* and Robert Sherwood. As fledgling editors at *Vanity Fair*, the magazine that was the darling of the sophisticated set, they shared an office and fell into the habit of lunching together every day. They chose the Algonquin because it was just up the street from their office and because the manager, Frank Case, a dapper hotelier with sweeping eyes and an innkeeper's hospitality, made them welcome.

Case's dining room was already a gathering place for actors and writers, so the trio from *Vanity Fair* were not alone. Friends gathered around them little by little. Before long, without anyone's trying to make it so, their gathering was an institution.

The Round Table's stock in trade was the barb, the blistering insult, delivered coolly to friend and foe alike, and the hero of the moment was the one who provided the last laugh, no matter at whose expense. To be a member one had to be invited; it was not a party to crash. But the membership swelled to some 30, of whom about 10 were generally present at lunch every day. Case, who liked them, treated them to free celery and popovers with their lunch and gave them a round table in the center of the room. Loving puns and thriving on insult, the lunchers called themselves the Vicious Circle, but when cartoonist Edmund Duffy caricatured them in the Brooklyn *Eagle* as knights at King Arthur's Round Table, he gave the wits the name by which celebrity-conscious New York came to know them.

They were in many ways an oddly assorted group. There was Alexander Woollcott *(opposite, upper right)*, the corpulent, owl-eyed arbiter of the theater, which he reviewed for the *Times*, resplendent in scarlet-lined opera cape. There was Franklin P. Adams, urbane and gargoyle-faced, whose "The Conning Tower" was perhaps the New York *World*'s most widely read column; to Adams went some of the credit for launching the younger Round Tablers on the path to celebrity, for he liberally laced his column with their bons mots (always attributed). There was George Kaufman *(opposite, lower right)*, gloomy and distant, who in collaboration with Marc Connelly and Edna Ferber, also Round Tablers, and a clutch of others, was to write 18 smash comedies for Broadway. There was columnist Heywood Broun, most disheveled of the lot, who called himself "an easy weeper." The only bleeding heart and reformer of the group, Broun spent the decade working to organize the New York Newspaper Guild, a task in which he finally succeeded after some 10 years. And there was Harold Ross *(opposite, upper left)*, said by Woollcott to look "like a dishonest Abe Lincoln." A man who could hardly tell a joke himself—when he tried he kept doubling over with laughter, punctuating his sentences with "See?"— Ross founded the brilliantly successful *New Yorker* magazine, which dealt with urbane humor, sophisticated fiction and the best reportage of the era.

When lunch was over on Saturday afternoons, the Round Table men adjourned upstairs, expanded their numbers and changed their name to the Thanatopsis Pleasure and Inside Straight Club, the object of which was to play marathon poker and tell more jokes. The name of the club was itself a joke, of course; it came from a do-gooding ladies' club in Sinclair Lewis' best-selling *Main Street*, where the Thanatopsians, cooed one of its members, "take such an interest in refinement and culture."

Women were not members of the Manhattan Thanatopsis, but they were welcome to kibitz and sometimes to play a hand. The games always went on through the afternoon and evening, sometimes all night, occasionally all weekend. Here, as at the Round Table, the humor, much of it ribald, rested on the pun and the insult. "I guess I'll fold up my tens and silently steal away," Woollcott once said. Adams accused early leavers of having "winner's sleeping sickness" and hangers-on of "loser's insomnia" or "Broun's disease"—named for Heywood, who used one coat pocket for his bank roll, another for his winnings, the better to tell when he broke even.

First Fig

My candle burns at both ends;
It will not last the night;
But ah, my foes, and oh, my friends—
It gives a lovely light!

Eel-grass

No matter what I say,
All that I really love
Is the rain that flattens on the bay,
And the eel-grass in the cove;
The jingle-shells that lie and bleach
At the tide-line, and the trace
Of higher tides along the beach:
Nothing in this place.

Feast

I drank at every vine.
The last was like the first.
I came upon no wine
So wonderful as thirst.

I gnawed at every root.
I ate of every plant.
I came upon no fruit
So wonderful as want.

Feed the grape and bean
To the vintner and monger;
I will lie down lean
With my thirst and my hunger.

Poet to an Era

Edna St. Vincent Millay was at once a rarity and a symbol for her time—a rarity because she achieved bestsellers writing poetry, a symbol because of her flippant air and carefree living. As a brand-new Vassar graduate, she arrived in New York "with a perfect passion for earning money," she wrote her mother, "don't care how I earn it." She earned it fast; her poetry so caught the public fancy that before long she was able to write home again that the magazines "just can't seem to go to press without me." Collected in books, her poetry sold in phenomenal quantities of a quarter million.

Voice of the Minority

Langston Hughes, a versatile black spokesman and stellar figure in the Negro Renaissance of the '20s, was first "discovered" by Vachel Lindsay. Hughes, a busboy in a Washington hotel where Lindsay was dining, placed a sheaf of papers by the great poet's plate, then fled. The next morning Hughes picked up a newspaper—and learned that Lindsay had not only admired his poems, but had admired them in the presence of reporters. Suddenly he was no longer obscure. Some months later publisher Alfred A. Knopf brought out Hughes's first book, *Weary Blues,* from which the excerpts at right are taken.

Afraid

We cry among the skyscrapers
As our ancestors
Cried among the palms in Africa
Because we are alone,
It is night,
And we're afraid.

Cabaret

Does a jazz-band ever sob?
They say a jazz-band's gay.
Yet as the vulgar dancers whirled
And the wan night wore away,
One said she heard the jazz-band sob
When the little dawn was grey.

Lament for Dark Peoples

I was a red man one time,
But the white men came.
I was a black man, too,
But the white men came.

They drove me out of the forest.
They took me away from the jungles.
I lost my trees.
I lost my silver moons.

Now they've caged me
In the circus of civilization.
Now I herd with the many
Caged in the circus of civilization.

Babbitt's Unexamined Life

Babbitt's virtues as a real-estate broker—as the servant of society in the department of finding homes for families and shops for distributors of food—were steadiness and diligence. Yet his eventual importance to mankind was perhaps lessened by his large and complacent ignorance of all architecture save the types of houses turned out by speculative builders; all landscape gardening save the use of curving roads, grass, and six ordinary shrubs; and all the commonest axioms of economics.

Though he did know the market-price, inch by inch, of certain districts of Zenith, he did not know whether the police force was too large or too small, or whether it was in alliance with gambling and prostitution. He knew the means of fire-proofing buildings and the relation of insurance-rates to fireproofing, but he did not know how many firemen there were in the city, how they were trained and paid, or how complete their apparatus. He sang eloquently the advantages of proximity of school-buildings to rentable homes, but he did not know—he did not know that it was worth while to know—whether the city schoolrooms were properly heated, lighted, ventilated, furnished; he did not know how the teachers were chosen; and though he chanted "One of the boasts of Zenith is that we pay our teachers adequately," that was because he had read the statement in the "Advocate-Times." Himself, he could not have given the average salary of teachers in Zenith or anywhere else.

A Slashing Novelist

Sinclair Lewis whipped up a maelstrom of controversy and adulation in 1920 with his novel *Main Street,* in which he trained his eagle eye on the shallow culture of provincial middle-class towns. Genteel traditionalists were outraged by the scorn that Lewis heaped upon his countrymen; others found his characters articulating a discontent that they were themselves beginning to feel. In quick succession Lewis published *Babbitt, Arrowsmith, Elmer Gantry* and *Dodsworth,* which together won their author the first Nobel Prize for Literature ever bestowed on an American. The excerpt at left is from *Babbitt.*

The Sage of Baltimore

Iconoclast Nonpareil

Democratic man is quite unable to think of himself as a free individual; he must belong to a group, or shake with fear and loneliness—and the group, of course, must have its leaders. It would be hard to find a country in which such brummagem serene highnesses are revered with more passionate devotion than they get in the United States. The distinction that goes with mere office runs far ahead of the distinction that goes with actual achievement. A Harding is regarded as superior to a Halsted, no doubt because his doings are better understood.

Sin is a dangerous toy in the hands of the virtuous. It should be left to the congenitally sinful, who know when to play with it and when to let it alone. Run a boy through a Presbyterian Sunday-school and you must police him carefully all the rest of his life, for once he slips he is ready for anything.

A boy with superabundant energy fogging him yearns for experiment and adventure. What he gets out of his teachers is mainly the opposite. On the female side they have the instincts of duennas, and on the male side they seldom rise above the level of scoutmasters and Y.M.C.A. secretaries. It would be hard enough for a grown man, with alcohol and cynicism aiding him, to endure such society. To a growing boy it is torture.

Henry Louis Mencken was the iconoclast nonpareil in an iconoclastic era, and the most prolific writer in a prolix time. Reporter, editor, critic, essayist, compiler, he aimed a barbed pen at every cranny of American life. His favorite targets were sham and hypocrisy, and as co-editor (with George Jean Nathan) of *The Smart Set* and *The American Mercury*, he made his name lambasting ministers, doctors, lawyers, Southern demagogues, educators, opponents of birth control and lovers of piety, all with Rabelaisian gusto. Warmly admired and hotly denounced, he was known as the "man who hates everything."

A Melancholy Dramatist

Eugene O'Neill raised American theater out of vaudeville and saccharine sentimentality, and won American drama its first serious notice abroad. This melancholy man, so nervous that he looked left and right when conversing and talked in his sleep of Freud, wrote upwards of 20 plays during this decade alone and earned Pulitzer Prizes for three, including *Anna Christie*, a drama about a relationship between a sailor and a prostitute *(excerpted below)*. His plays, which appeared in theaters from Moscow to Buenos Aires, are as somber as their author's face, dealing with insanity, murder, suicide and death. The excerpt at right is from an article he wrote for the New York *Tribune* in February 1921.

A Different Kind of Protagonist

Burke (throwing the chair away into a corner of the room— helplessly): I can't do it, God help me, and your two eyes looking at me. (furiously) Though I do be thinking I've have a good right to smash your skull like a rotten egg. Was there iver a woman in the world had the rottenness in her that you have, and was ther iver a man the like of me was made the fool of the world, and me thinking thoughts about you, and having great love for you, and dreaming dreams of the fine life we'd have when we'd be wedded! (his voice high pitched in a lamentation that is like a keen) Yerra, God help me! I'm destroyed entirely and my heart is broken in bits! I'm asking God Himself, was it for this He'd have me roaming the earth since I was a lad only, to come to black shame in the end, where I'd be giving a power of love to a woman is the same as others you'd meet in any hooker-shanty in port, with red gowns on them and paint on their grinning mugs, would be sleeping with any man for a dollar or two!

Anna (in a scream): Don't, Mat! For Gawd's sake! (then raging and pounding on the table with her hands) Get out of here! Leave me alone! Get out of here!

Burke (his anger rushing back on him): I'll be going, surely! And I'll be drinking sloos of whiskey will wash that black kiss of yours off my lips; and I'll be getting dead rotten drunk so I'll not remember if 'twas iver born you was at all; and I'll be shipping away on some boat will take me to the other end of the world where I'll never see your face again! (He turns toward the door.)

Chris (who has been standing in a stupor—suddenly grasping Burke by the arm—stupidly): No, you don't go. Ay tank maybe it's better Anna marry you now.

Burke (shaking Chris off—furiously): Lave go of me, ye old ape! Marry her, is it? I'd see her roasting in hell first! I'm shipping away out of this, I'm telling you! (pointing to Anna—passionately) And my curse on you and the curse of Almighty God and all the Saints! You've destroyed me this day and may you lie awake in the long nights, tormented with thoughts of Mat Burke and the great wrong you've done him!

Anna (in anguish): Mat! (but he turns without another word and strides out of the doorway. Anna looks after him wildly, starts to run after him, then hides her face in her outstretched arms, sobbing. Chris stands in a stupor, staring at the floor.)

Chris (after a pause, dully): Ay tank Ay go ashore, too.

I have been accused of unmitigated gloom. Is this a pessimistic view of life? I do not think so. There is a skin deep optimism and another higher optimism, not skin deep, which is usually confounded with pessimism. To me, the tragic alone has that significant beauty which is truth. It is the meaning of life—and the hope. The noblest is eternally the most tragic. The people who succeed and do not push on to a greater failure are the spiritual middle classers. Their stopping at success is the proof of their compromising insignificance. How pretty their dreams must have been! The man who pursues the mere attainable should be sentenced to get it—and keep it. Let him rest on his laurels and enthrone him in a Morris chair, in which laurels and hero may wither away together. Only through the unattainable does man achieve a hope worth living and dying for—and so attain himself. He with the spiritual guerdon of a hope in hopelessness, is nearest to the stars and the rainbow's foot.

Damn the optimists anyway! They make life so darned hopeless!

Names in the News

It was an era when anyone whose name was in the newspapers was automatically a celebrity. Whether the publicity was wanted or not, whether the person in question was a scientist, cellist, senator or murderer—it didn't make any difference. The press and the radio were talking, and in the eyes of the public that person had been touched with magic.

People felt they were on a first-name basis with Edward, Prince of Wales, and Queen Marie of Romania (both of whom paid splashy visits to the United States), and everyone everywhere discussed Albert Einstein's absentmindedness as though he were a neighbor. The man on the street referred casually to the way the great financier Bernard Baruch was playing the stock market or what Paris gowns the Vanderbilt ladies were buying. Evangelists like Billy Sunday and Aimee Semple McPherson, pilots like Eddie Rickenbacker, society playgirls like Peggy Hopkins Joyce, even Freud and advice-to-the-lovelorn columnist Dorothy Dix—all were known quantities, recognizable personalities, friendly faces.

One way for a public figure to make it big was to be—or appear to be—particularly average. Hiram Wesley Evans, the Imperial Wizard of the Ku Klux Klan, declared proudly that he was "the most average man in America," but there were many others fiercely competing for that distinction. One contender in mid-decade was the President, Calvin Coolidge. In an age that was loud, extravagant and zany, the President was silent, frugal and drab. The son of a Vermont farmer, he seldom spoke in public (though his intimates said he was a maddening chatter-box in private) and he wore an expression that one quipster said suggested he had been "weaned on a pickle."

The prestige of the "average" man, however, took a serious beating in 1925 during the famous "Monkey Trial" in Dayton, Tennessee. The state of Tennessee had passed a law against teaching the theory of evolution in the public schools. (The theory was commonly—and wrongly—expressed by its detractors as holding that "man was descended from a monkey.") When a local teacher, John T. Scopes, was accused of breaking the law, Clarence Darrow, a famous lawyer, an agnostic and a champion of civil liberties, volunteered to defend him. The state was represented by William Jennings Bryan, a Fundamentalist who had been defeated three times as the Democratic candidate for the Presidency. Bryan liked to think he stood for the average man and relished his sobriquet, "The Great Commoner." The high point of the trial came when Darrow cross-examined Bryan about his religious beliefs. Bryan affirmed his literal interpretation of the Bible—that the world was created in 4004 B.C., that Jonah was swallowed by a big fish, that Eve was made out of Adam's rib. Bryan claimed that the purpose of the examination was "to cast ridicule on everybody who believes in the Bible," to which Darrow replied in a withering attack: "We have the purpose of preventing bigots and ignoramuses from controlling the education of the United States."

The Court convicted Scopes and the Tennesseeans applauded Bryan, but much of the world shook with laughter over the spectacle Bryan had made of himself. Bryan's notion that one honest, average man was worth a handful of experts had suffered a devastating blow, and soon after the trial "The Great Commoner" died, a shattered man.

Calvin Coolidge

A man with a flair for publicity, President Coolidge frequently made appearances rigged out in Indian feathers or cowboy clothes. Coolidge succeeded Warren G. Harding in office and sought to free his administration of the scandals that had plagued Harding. A Republican and a conservative, he once said that government's "greatest duty and opportunity is not to embark on any new ventures."

Richard E. Byrd

Resplendent in his uniform, Byrd rides with New York's official greeter, Grover Whalen, through a storm of ticker tape in 1930, after the explorer's return from a year in Antarctica. While there, Byrd commanded the first flight over the South Pole and had radioed The New York Times at the moment he passed over it. The Navy made him a Rear Admiral and Congress struck a medal in his honor.

Marcus Garvey

On his way to a Madison Square Garden rally for the Universal Negro Improvement Association, black leader Marcus Garvey wears the uniform he had devised as "Provisional President of Africa." Garvey raised millions of dollars to finance his scheme to help black Americans emigrate to Africa. But in 1923 he was convicted for using the mails illegally and was sentenced to prison.

Will Rogers

Part Cherokee Indian, an Oklahoma cowboy and America's favorite comedian, Will Rogers cracked jokes in his slow drawl on the stage, on the radio and in the movies and wrote a news-paper column. When invited to fly, Rogers referred to his flight uniform as "a one-piece suicide suit" and later remarked, "Here I was thousands of feet up in the air when you can't even get me to ride a tall horse."

Billy Mitchell

A fiery advocate of U.S. air power, Brigadier General Billy Mitchell flew for the Army in World War I. During the '20s he championed an independent air force. When his plea was repeatedly ignored, Mitchell accused his superiors of being "incompetent, criminally negligent and almost treasonable." For this he was court-martialed and suspended on half pay, where-upon he resigned from the Army.

Alfred E. Smith

While running for the Presidency in 1928, Alfred E. Smith stopped off at a Boy Scout camp near New York City and was presented with an outsized version of his campaign symbol, the brown derby. Though Smith, the first Catholic to try for the Presidency, lost to Republican Herbert Hoover, he retained his popularity in New York, where he served four terms as governor between 1919 and 1928.

Jimmy Walker

Tiny Jimmy Walker, New York's affable mayor (above, left), dons a ten-gallon hat to greet popular Hollywood cowboy Tom Mix. Costumes were Walker's strong point; he usually changed clothes three times a day. Though he neglected city affairs during his regime, the New Yorker commented: "Walker does things of infinitely greater importance. He lives. He is carefree, obviously happy."

William Jennings Bryan

On the afternoon of July 20, 1925, in a Dayton, Tennessee, courtroom, the career of William Jennings Bryan (at left in picture) ended with a whimper. A golden orator, Presidential candidate, and defender of the faith, Bryan had lately turned himself into the Don Quixote of a bygone rural American age, playing the role of Bible expert as a witness against evolution in the Scopes trial. For an hour and a half, sweating and shouting under the baiting of defense counsel Clarence Darrow, he spouted Fundamentalisms and contradicted himself. He left the stand exhausted and discredited.

Clarence Darrow

Social philosopher, agnostic, free spirit, Clarence Darrow (far right) was a man who chose to become involved, who cared and who gave of himself. The great lawyer defended unpopular causes and persons; and his defense of John T. Scopes, undertaken without pay, was wholly in character. So was the fact that after he had savaged Bryan he felt sorry for the lonely old man; Darrow was a tough, clever man, but one with love. In 1922 Edgar Lee Masters wrote about his former law partner: "There were tears for human suffering, or for a glance into the vast futility of life."

The Glamour of the Films

In an age of celebrities, the most glamorous of all were the movie stars. In the earliest days of film, producers had tried to keep their actors anonymous lest they become popular and demand huge salaries. But by the '20s the moviemakers had come to realize that a big name outdrew a good picture—and was worth big money. Soon a major attraction like Lillian Gish could ask for $400,000 a year.

By 1920 some 35 million Americans were going to the movies at least once a week, mainly to see melodramatic love stories and Westerns; in 1926 the first war films began to appear; and in 1927 gangster pictures started their vogue. The top movie personalities—whether they were cowboys, vamps, flappers, comedians, cops, robbers or swashbucklers—were now receiving about 32 million fan letters a year.

Every aspect of the stars' lives was followed with fascination. The marriage of Mary Pickford to Douglas Fairbanks in 1920 set off nationwide jubilation. When Charlie Chaplin visited England a year later, the British lined the docks to welcome him. Even animal stars were idolized; the dog Rin-Tin-Tin was voted most popular film performer in 1926. Perhaps the most fascinating of all the stars, however, was the publicity-shy Swedish actress Greta Garbo. She was so elusive and standoffish that studio press agents at first complained about how uncooperative she was being. Soon, however, it became clear that her very insistence on privacy was an enormous asset, and the legend of Garbo "The Sphinx" was launched.

Greta Garbo inspired such devotion that her fans were called "Garbomaniacs."

Rudolph Valentino, most famous of the screen lovers, gives a sulky pout in his next-to-last role, as Dubrovski in The Eagle.

The Hollywood Sex Queens

Alla Nazimova invested her life savings to produce Salome.

Pola Negri, exotic and hot-tempered, dances in Bella Donna.

Gloria Swanson flirts in Her Gilded Cage, a 1922 tearjerker.

Ziegfeld Girl Mae Murray was a glittering Merry Widow.

The Lovers

Dolores Costello and John Barrymore appeared together in Sea Beast.

*An intense Rudolph Valentino
embraces Alla Nozimova.*

*Janet Gaynor and Charles
Farrell starred in Seventh
Heaven, a 1927 film.*

Greta Garbo and John Gilbert make love in Flesh and the Devil, *which established her as a star.*

The younger set: Douglas Fairbanks Jr. and Joan Crawford.

Vilma Banky and Ronald Colman act the title roles in Two Lovers.

Great Comedians of a Slapstick Era

Harold Lloyd (left), perched precariously on a clock above the street, flirts with danger in Safety Last.

Buster Keaton (opposite), who never smiled on screen, bathes in a scene from The Three Ages, in which he was cast as a prehistoric cave man.

Forlorn and cold, Charlie Chaplin (right) huddles by his shack in The Gold Rush.

Fads and Ballyhoo

CRAZES THAT CAPTURED THE NATION

Long-distance dancers tango from Santa Monica to Los Angeles.

Fame, Fortune, and Folly

During the '20s Americans were torn by two contrary desires: the urge to be like everyone else, and the urge to be utterly different. For many people, both yearnings were neatly satisfied by the zany fads that swept the country during the decade. By taking up the latest craze, an American could demonstrate that he was a good conformist. On the other hand, by being a little more fad-happy than his neighbors—by becoming the local expert on mah-jongg rules or the best at doing crossword puzzles or the most indefatigable marathon dancer—he could prove that he really was unlike anyone else, unique in his chosen field.

In previous decades, the pace of pop culture had been more measured; fads and habits had changed, but only very gradually. During the '20s, however, the advent of nationwide radio networks and the growing use of syndicated columns helped to disseminate with whirlwind speed news of the most recent parlor game or endurance contest. Simultaneously, publicists perfected ways of focusing the full glare of the mass media on their pet projects.

Crossword puzzles were a prime example. Two young publishers, Richard L. Simon and M. Lincoln Schuster, brought out a collection of the puzzles as their first book. Skillful promoters, Simon and Schuster attached pencils to each volume, devised an ingenious advertising campaign—and watched their profits soar. Suddenly everyone was crazy about crosswords. The Baltimore and Ohio Railroad placed dictionaries on trains for the convenience of puzzlers. College teams competed in tournaments and in New York thousands of fans cheered two crossword finalists in a national contest. The University of Kentucky offered a course in crossword puzzles because, as the dean said, they were "educational, scientific, instructive and mentally stimulative, as well as entertaining."

Crosswords were just one of scores of fads that swept the country. Contract bridge, yo-yo's and roller-skating became popular manias. People competed in rocking-chair derbies, dance marathons and cross-country races. Others hoped to win fleeting fame by becoming the world's champion pea-eater or kisser or talker. A man in Minnesota claimed a world's record after he bobbed up and down in the water 1,843 times, prompting *The Saturday Evening Post* to comment wryly that Americans were "first in war, first in peace, first in tree sitting, gum chewing, peanut pushing and bobbing up and down in water."

"Clarence Tillman, 17, local high school student, put 40 sticks of chewing gum in his mouth at one time, sang "Home, Sweet Home," and between verses of the song, drank a gallon of milk."

United Press Dispatch from Warsaw, Indiana

Pursuing a great fad of the era, a woman looks up "Egyptian Sun God" in the world's smallest crossword-puzzle dictionary, strapped to her wrist.

Flagpole Sitting

"Shipwreck" Kelly (above) sways above a theater in Union City, New Jersey.

T he Luckiest Fool Alive," as he called himself, was "Shipwreck" Kelly, the era's most famous flagpole sitter. A former boxer who fought under the name Sailor Kelly, he was knocked out so often that fans started shouting, "The sailor's been shipwrecked again"—thus, his nickname.

Shipwreck started sitting on flagpoles in 1924 in Hollywood, where a theater had hired him to draw crowds. Soon he was booked by scores of hotels desiring publicity. Balanced on a small disk equipped with stirrups to keep him from falling off, Kelly took five-minute catnaps every hour and subsisted on liquids hoisted up to him on ropes. In 1929 Kelly put in a total of 145 days on various flagpoles.

All that was lacking in Shipwreck's career was romance—and that came to him one day in Dallas when a hotel elevator girl indignantly slapped a passenger who called Kelly a fool. Kelly, sitting on the hotel's flagpole, asked to meet the 18-year-old girl. She was hoisted up for a chat; after he came down they were married. Six years later the girl sued for a divorce, charging that his career had come between them. "What's the use of having a husband," she asked the judge, "unless he comes home nights?"

Despite such minor setbacks, Shipwreck's fame continued to grow, and many imitators sprang up—particularly, for some reason, in Baltimore. The Baltimore flagpole madness began when 15-year-old Avon Foreman set up an 18-foot hickory sapling in his back yard and perched on top. Others followed suit, and during one week in 1929 Baltimore had no fewer than 20 pole-sitters (17 boys and 3 girls). The city's proud mayor visited many of the arboreal Baltimoreans and even sent a letter to young Avon Foreman, congratulating him for his accomplishment.

Baltimore's pride, Avon Foreman sits on a platform that he mounted on a pole. During his feat, he received encouragement from some 5,000 neighbors.

The Mah-Jongg Craze

In 1922 an ancient Chinese game called mah-jongg invaded America. By the following year millions of people, particularly members of ladies' clubs, were shouting "Pung!" and "Chow!" and other exotic words at one another. Many enthusiasts refused to play without the proper accessories, and sales of Chinese robes soared.

A sort of combination of dice and dominoes, mah-jongg required a set of 144 tiles, originally manufactured only in China. In 1923 mah-jongg sets outsold radios; the demand was so great that the Chinese ran out of the shinbones of calves, which were used to make the tiles. The beef-packers of Chicago had to ship bones from their slaughterhouses to China so that artisans there could carve them into tiles and then send them back to the United States. American efficiency experts also helped the Chinese set up mah-jongg assembly lines. A good set manufactured in China might sell in the U.S. for as much as $500, although American-made copies fashioned in celluloid could be bought for only a few dollars.

The game's notorious complexities were satirized by Eddie Cantor, who sang in the revue *Kid Boots* a song titled "Since Ma Is Playing Mah Jong." One stanza went:

> If you want to play the game I'll tell you what to do,
> Buy a silk kimona and begin to raise a queue;
> Get yourself a book of rules and study till it's clear,
> And you'll know the game when you've got whiskers down to here.

As the song implies, the rules of play, also made in China, were inscrutable and subject to change. During the decade more than 20 rule books were issued, often at variance with one another. On the West Coast, where the game was particularly popular, the *Seattle Daily Times* printed a mah-jongg column in which new rule interpretations were offered. One rule book complained that the game was being ruined by "expert" instructors who made up regulations as they went along. "Even the Chinese in America are not without reproach," the book said, "for certain of them have posed as professional teachers although their acquaintance with the game has been of shorter duration than that of many Americans."

Decked out in Oriental finery, a galaxy of film starlets gathers around a mah-jongg table at "the shrine of the Chinese God of Luck" in Los Angeles.

Starting pistol ready, a promoter prepares to launch a marathon in Dallas. The tidiness of the contestants demonstrates that the event has not yet begun.

The Dance of Exhaustion

O f all the crazy competitions ever invented," the New York *World* remarked in 1923, "the dancing marathon wins by a considerable margin of lunacy." The object of these strange contests was to see which couple could outdance—or outlive—all the others. All across the country men and women staggered in near-exhaustion to the tune of fox trots played by Victrolas or seedy little bands.

The dancers sometimes competed for prizes of as much as several thousand dollars. The spectators came to see the antics of the performers. In order to keep their partners awake, dancers would kick and punch them and offer them smelling salts and ice packs. Unprincipled contestants would slip their rivals drinks containing sleeping pills or laxatives. After seven or eight days of painful plodding (in 1930 a Chicago marathon went on for 119 days) dancers would often start acting peculiarly. Girls would come to hate their partners so much they would scream when they saw them. One man in New York suffered from delusions that someone was picking his pocket; he was disqualified when he ran off the floor and down the street chasing an imaginary culprit.

One of the few contestants who never seemed to suffer from mental problems or aching feet was Mary "Hercules" Promitis of Pittsburgh. Learning that bare-fisted prize fighters often pickled their hands, Hercules soaked her feet in brine and vinegar for three weeks before a 1928 Madison Square Garden marathon. So successful was the method that when the New York health commissioner finally ended the dance, after three weeks, Mary was still feeling no pain.

An orderly administers to a dancer who has collapsed at a marathon in Los Angeles (above right). Many contestants died of heart failure during marathons.

"There is nothing inspiring in seeing an extremely tired pretty girl in a worn bathrobe, dingy white stockings in rolls about scuffing felt slippers, her eyes half shut, her arms hung over her partner's shoulders, drag aching feet that seemed glued to the floor in one short, agonizing step after another."

New York *World,* 1923

Here She Comes—Miss America!

In 1921 the first contest to select a Miss America was held in Atlantic City and it epitomized the hokum of the '20s. First of all, it was a money-making scheme devised by the town fathers and local newsmen to promote the resort; the pageant was staged immediately after Labor Day as an effort to keep tourists in town and the hotels full. Secondly, the competition became immensely popular because it promised to take an ordinary, good-looking girl and turn her into a celebrity; Americans everywhere were pleased by the notion that through the contest some Little Miss Nobody could achieve instant distinction and become an idolized Somebody.

The first contest was a modest affair. Only eight girls entered and most of the public attention centered on the judge, or "King Neptune," who was Hudson Maxim of the armaments-inventing Maxims. By 1924, however, 83 girls were competing, and by 1927 the festivities had become an exhausting, week-long bore. On the first day the girls (who then represented cities rather than states) endured a long official greeting and lunch with the local Rotary Club. On the second day they went to a rehearsal in the morning, viewed a Baby and Juvenile Parade in the afternoon (a prize was given for the cutest child aged two to six) and, in the evening, attended a ball. On the third morning the girls participated in a bathing-suit contest—attired, by official decree, in Annette Kellerman bathing suits. That afternoon they rode in decorated floats, this time donning the mandatory "Fancy Silk Celanese Violet Ray Bathing Suit." In the evening they competed for the title of "Most Beautiful Girl in Evening Gown" (no manufacturer specified). On the fourth day Miss America was finally selected from among the exhausted contestants. In the afternoon there was another dreary parade and that evening yet another event—the Coronation.

The contestants were so harassed and exploited that after 1924 Trenton, New Jersey, refused to send any more candidates. The Trenton *Evening Times,* which had sponsored the previous year's contestant, wrote the director of the contest an indignant letter complaining of the treatment she had received: "We had assured 'Miss Trenton' a week in Atlantic City that would include abundant time to enjoy the bathing, the promenading advantages of the Boardwalk and other pleasant phases of social life. She was never given time during the progress of the tournament to take a dip in the ocean or a stroll on the Boardwalk. The program laid out by your committee not only seriously taxed the physical strength of 'Miss Trenton' but there was also manifested no apparent consideration for the natural modesty of the young women who participated." The *Times* was not alone in its concern for the morals of girls who paraded in swimsuits in front of men, as is demonstrated by the articles excerpted below.

Charging that the Atlantic City bathing beauty parade exposed the young women participants to serious perils, the Directors of the Young Women's Christian Association adopted a resolution today condemning the annual fete. "The board has felt for a long time that such contests are harmful in every way," the letter says. "The notoriety is unsettling. The girls are exposed to grave dangers from unscrupulous persons, and the shocking costumes which such contests encourage certainly call for protests from organizations interested in girls' welfare."
–Atlantic City Press, April 19, 1924

Nowadays some of the resorts seem to have adopted a form of advertising which combines a maximum amount of sophistication with a minimum amount of brains and imagination. We can think of nothing better designed to develop a false point of view in the minds of the youthful contestants for these beauty prizes than the notoriety which is given to them in the press and film. These contests lack the wholesomeness of almost any kind of athletic contest, for victory is given for something which has no relation to achievement or skill.
–The Outlook, September 10, 1924

King Neptune presents Ruth Malcolmson, 1924 winner, with her victor's crown and trophy.

Wearing the banners of their cities, Miss America contestants—including the ultimate winner, Miss Philadelphia—line up for review in 1924.

ACKNOWLEDGMENTS

The editors of this book wish to thank the following persons and institutions for their assistance:

The Academy of Motion Picture Arts and Sciences, Hollywood; Sid Albright, Information Bureau Manager, Western Airlines; Natalie Andrews, Assistant, Photographic Archives, University of Louisville; Frances Bearden, Fondren Library, Southern Methodist University; Jerry Berns, "21" Club, New York; Amelia D. Bielaski, Curator, Smith-Telfer Collection, New York State Historical Association, Cooperstown, New York; The Boeing Company, Seattle; Paul Bonner Jr., The Condé Nast Publications Inc., New York; Margery Booker, Chamber of Commerce, San Francisco; Larry Booth, Director of Historical Collection, Title Insurance and Trust Company, San Diego; Ruth P. Braun, *The Detroit News,* Detroit; Mrs. Robert Crowe, Playa del Rey, California; Virginia Daiker, Prints and Photographs Division, Library of Congress; Alice Dalligan, Curator of Manuscripts, Burton Historical Collection, Detroit Public Library; James Davis, Librarian, Western History Department, Denver Public Library; Leslie R. Diveley, Columbia, Missouri; Frank Driggs, New York; Edholm and Blomgren, Photographers, Lincoln, Nebraska; Ruth K. Field, Curator of Pictures, Missouri Historical Society, St. Louis; Hannah D. French, Wellesley College Library, Wellesley, Massachusetts; Estelle Galbreath, Piggly Wiggly Corporation, Jacksonville, Florida; Dorothy Gimmestad, Acting Curator, Picture Department, Minnesota Historical Society, St. Paul; Henry Graham, San Antonio; Ben Hall, New York; Gita Hall, Warner-Lambert Pharmaceutical Company, New York; Dale Hoaglan, KMTV, Omaha; Orrin Keepnews, Milestone Records, New York; Dick Lemen, East Moline, Illinois; David Lighthall, editor, *Chainstore Age,* New York; Ed Matthews, Piggly Wiggly Corporation, Jacksonville, Florida; Jo and Fred Mazulla, Denver; Robert D. Monroe, Chief of Special Collections, University of Washington Library, Seattle; Joseph E. Molloy, Librarian, *Philadelphia Inquirer,* Philadelphia; Mrs. Nickolas Muray, New York; Daniel Murphy, Leslie Jones Collection, *The Boston Herald,* Boston; Museum of the City of New York; Kathleen Pierson, State Historical Society of Colorado, Denver; Victor R. Plukas, Bank Historian, Security Pacific National Bank, Los Angeles; Ruth Revels, Local History Department, Milwaukee Public Library; Norman Rogers, Dallas; Gleason Wait Romer, Miami; Meyer Rosen, News Bureau Chief, *Los Angeles Times,* Los Angeles; Winthrop Sears Jr., Henry Ford Museum, Dearborn, Michigan; Irving Settel, New York; Bertha Stratford, Museum of History and Industry, Seattle; Ray Stuart, Hollywood, California; Patrick Sullivan, Library of the Commonwealth of Massachusetts, Boston; Judith Topaz, Assistant, Iconographic Collections, State Historical Society of Wisconsin, Madison; Mary Wotring, Head of Archives, Columbia Records, New York.

PICTURE CREDITS

BIBLIOGRAPHY

Abels, Jules, *In the Time of Silent Cal.* G. P. Putnam's Sons, 1969.

Allen, Frederick Lewis, *Only Yesterday.* Harper & Row, 1964.

Asbury, Herbert, *The Great Illusion.* Doubleday & Company, Inc., 1950.

Bird, Caroline, *The Invisible Scar.* David McKay Co., 1966.

Churchill, Allen, *Remember When.* Golden Press, Inc., 1967.

Daniels, Jonathan, *The Time Between the Wars.* Doubleday & Company, 1966.

Danzig, Allison and Brandwein, Peter, eds., *Sport's Golden Age.* Harper & Brothers, 1948.

Dulles, Foster R., *Twentieth Century America.* Houghton Mifflin Co., 1945.

Earnest, Ernest, *Academic Procession.* The Bobbs-Merrill Company, Inc., 1953.

Franklin, Joe, *Classics of the Silent Screen.* The Citadel Press, 1959.

Galbraith, John Kenneth, *The Great Crash: 1929.* Houghton Mifflin Co., 1955.

Hall, Ben M., *The Best Remaining Seats.* Clarkson N. Potter, Inc., 1961.

Harriman, Margaret Chase, *The Vicious Circle.* Rinehart & Company, 1951.

Johnston, Alva, *The Legendary Mizners.* Farrar, Straus and Young, 1953.

Merz, Charles, *The Dry Decade.* Doubleday, Doran & Company, 1931.

Ramsey, Frederick Jr. and Smith, Charles E., eds., *Jazzmen.* Harcourt, Brace, 1939.

Russell, Francis, *The Shadow of Blooming Grove.* McGraw-Hill Book Co., 1968.

Sann, Paul, *Fads, Follies and Delusions of the American People.* Crown Publishers, Inc., 1967.

The Lawless Decade. Crown Publishers, Inc., 1957.

Settel, Irving, *A Pictorial History of Radio.* Grossett & Dunlap, 1967.

Shapiro, Nat and Hentoff, Nat, eds., *Hear Me Talkin' To Ya.* Rinehart & Co., 1955.

Sinclair, Andrew, *Prohibition, The Era of Excess.* Little, Brown and Company, 1962.

Slosson, Preston W., *The Great Crusade and After: 1914–1928.* The Macmillan Company, 1930.

Stevenson, Elizabeth, *Babbitts and Bohemians: The American 1920s.* The Macmillan Company, 1967.

Sullivan, Mark, *Our Times. Vol. 6, The Twenties.* Charles Scribner's Sons, 1937.

Walker, Stanley, *The Night Club Era.* Frederick A. Stokes Company, 1933.

Wood, James P., *The Story of Advertising.* Ronald Press Co., 1958.

TEXT CREDITS

25: Lippmann quote from *A Preface to Morals* by Walter Lippmann. Macmillan Co., 1929, p. 17. **41:** Fitzgerald on New York from *Scott Fitzgerald* by Andrew Turnbull. Charles Scribner's Sons, 1962, p. 183. **77:** De Forest quote from *The Story of Advertising* by James Playsted Wood. The Ronald Press Company, 1958, p. 414. **96:** Rice, from New York *Sun*, September 29, 1930. Keeler, from *Yesterday in Sports*, ed. by John Durant. A.S. Barnes and Company, 1956, pp. 99–100. **114:** From *The Night Club Era* by Stanley Walker. Frederick A. Stokes Company, 1933, pp. 288–289. **118:** Einstein, from *Prohibition Agent No. 1* by Izzy Einstein. Frederick A. Stokes Company, 1932, p. 14. **150:** "Eel-Grass," "First Fig" and "Feast": From *Collected Poems* by Edna St. Vincent Millay, edited by Norma Millay. Harper & Row Publishers, pp. 68, 127, 158. © 1921, 1922, 1923; renewed 1948, 1950, 1951. Used by permission of Norma Millay Ellis. **151:** "Cabaret," "Lament for Dark Peoples" and "Afraid": From *The Weary Blues* by Langston Hughes. © 1926 and renewed 1954 by Langston Hughes. Reprinted by permission of Alfred A. Knopf, Inc., pp. 29, 100, 101. **152:** From *Babbitt* by Sinclair Lewis. © 1922 by Harcourt, Brace & World Inc.; renewed 1950 by Sinclair Lewis, pp. 42–43. Reprinted by permission of publishers. **153:** "Democratic man": © 1926 and renewed 1954 by H. L. Mencken. Reprinted from *The Vintage Mencken*, Gathered by Alistair Cooke, by permission of Alfred A. Knopf, Inc., p. 175. "A boy" and "Sin": From *The Vintage Mencken*, Gathered by Alistair Cooke. © 1955 by Alfred A. Knopf, Inc., pp. 183, 187–188. Reprinted by permission of the publisher. **155:** From *O'Neill and His Plays* edited by Oscar Cargill, N.B. Fagin and W. J. Fisher. New York University Press, 1961, pp. 104, 106. *Anna Christie:* From *Four Plays by Eugene O'Neill,* introduction by A.R. Gurney. Penguin Group, 1998, pp. 224–225.

INDEX

Time-Life Books is a division of Time Life Inc.

TIME LIFE INC.
PRESIDENT and CEO: George Artandi

TIME-LIFE BOOKS
PUBLISHER/MANAGING EDITOR: Neil Kagan
SENIOR VICE PRESIDENT, MARKETING: Joseph A. Kuna
VICE PRESIDENT, NEW PRODUCT DEVELOPMENT:
Amy Golden

OUR AMERICAN CENTURY
The Jazz Age: The 20s

EDITORS: Loretta Britten, Paul Mathless
DIRECTOR, NEW PRODUCT DEVELOPMENT:
Elizabeth D. Ward
DIRECTOR OF MARKETING: Pamela R. Farrell

Deputy Editor: Charles J. Hagner
Photo Coordinator: Betty H. Weatherley
Editorial Assistant: Christine Higgins

Design for **Our American Century** by Antonio Alcalá,
Studio A, Alexandria, Virginia.

Correspondents: Maria Vincenza Aloisi (Paris), Christine Hinze
(London), Christina Lieberman (New York).

Director of Finance: Christopher Hearing
Directors of Book Production: Marjann Caldwell, Patricia Pascale
Director of Publishing Technology: Betsi McGrath
Director of Photography and Research: John Conrad Weiser
Director of Editorial Administration: Barbara Levitt
Manager, Technical Services: Anne Topp
Senior Production Manager: Ken Sabol
Production Manager: Virginia Reardon
Quality Assurance Manager: James King
Chief Librarian: Louise D. Forstall

The Jazz Age was produced by Bishop Books, Inc., New York.

This revised edition was originally published as
THIS FABULOUS CENTURY: 1920–1930.

EDITORIAL CONSULTANT
Richard B. Stolley is currently senior editorial adviser at Time
Inc. After 19 years at *Life* magazine as a reporter, bureau chief,
and assistant managing editor, he became the first managing
editor of *People* magazine, a position he held with great success
for eight years. He then returned to *Life* magazine as managing
editor and later served as editorial director for all Time Inc.
magazines. In 1997 Stolley received the Henry Johnson Fisher
Award for Lifetime Achievement, the magazine industry's
highest honor.

Library of Congress Cataloging-in-Publication Data
The jazz age: the 20s / by the editors of Time-Life Books.
    p. cm. — (Our American century)
Includes bibliographical references and index.
ISBN 0-7835-5509-1
1. United States—History—1919–1933.
2. Nineteen twenties.
3. United States—History—1919–1933—Pictorial works.
4. Nineteen twenties—Pictorial works.
5. Jazz—1921–1930—History and criticism.
I. Time-Life Books.   II. Series.
E784.J39 1998
973.91—dc21   98-33969
                                         CIP
                                         MN

Other History Publications:

World War II	Lost Civilizations
What Life Was Like	Mysteries of the Unknown
The American Story	Time Frame
Voices of the Civil War	The Civil War
The American Indians	Cultural Atlas

For information on and a full description of any of
the Time-Life Books series listed above, please call
1-800-621-7026 or write:
Reader Information
Time-Life Customer Service
P.O. Box C-32068
Richmond, Virginia 23261-2068

On the cover: Rosie and Jenny Dolly—born Roszika and Yancsi
Dutsch—were identical twins from Hungary who became
darlings of the vaudeville circuit as the Dolly Sisters. They
epitomized the '20s—stylish, elegant, and forever focused on
simply having fun. Other figures from the '20s are pictured
from left to right at the top: poet Langston Hughes, gangster
Al Capone, blues singer Bessie Smith, aviator Charles
Lindbergh, poet Edna St. Vincent Millay, and football player
Red Grange. Baseball legend Babe Ruth appears on the spine.